The Complete Handbook of Advanced Multi-Purpose Offensive Basketball Drills

Burrall Paye and Patrick Paye

COACHES CHOICE™

ISBN: 978-1-58518-068-4
Library of Congress Control Number: 2007938971
Cover design: Roger W. Rybkowski
Book layout: Roger W. Rybkowski
Front cover photo: Geoff Burke/USP/ZUMA Press

Coaches Choice
P.O. Box 1828
Monterey, CA 93942
www.coacheschoice.com

Contents

How to Use This Book 7
Drills Finder 10
Two Drills to Illustrate 16
    Drill #1: Fivo 17
    Drill #2: Crashing the Boards 19

Chapter 1: Shooting 21
    Drill #3: Full-Court Shooting Contest
    Drill #4: Post Shooting
    Drill #5: Six-Basket Shooting
    Drill #6: Six-Basket Shooting Contest
    Drill #7: Post Shooting and Conditioning
    Drill #8: Full-Court Golf Shooting Game
    Drill #9: Six Teams Rotating
    Drill #10: Three-Line Shooting Game
    Drill #11: Individual Reaction Shooting
    Drill #12: Team Three-Point Shooting
    Drill #13: Pressure Shooting
    Drill #14: Full-Court Shooting and Conditioning
    Drill #15: Speed Shooting
    Drill #16: No-Rim Shooting

Chapter 2: Passing 39
    Drill #17: Team Sprint Passing
    Drill #18: Outlet Pass and Shooting
    Drill #19: Touch Passing
    Drill #20: Post Pepper Passing
    Drill #21: Shooting, Passing, and Touch Passing
    Drill #22: Passing and Slide Step
    Drill #23: Wall Passing
    Drill #24: Skip Passing and Shooting
    Drill #25: Baseball Pass and Dribbling Lay-Up
    Drill #26: Fake Passing
    Drill #27: Spectrum Passing
    Drill #28: Diamond Passing
    Drill #29: Four-Corner Passing
    Drill #30: Two-Player Rapid Fire
    Drill #31: Team Post Passing
    Drill #32: Two-on-One Passing
    Drill #33: Combo Overhead and Chest Passing
    Drill #34: Pepper Passing

Chapter 3: Dribbling 61

Drill #35: Advanced Dribble Slap

Drill #36: Full-Court Recovery

Drill #37: Skip Pass and Penetration

Drill #38: Dribble, Pivot, and Pass Team

Drill #39: Recovery Lay-Up

Drill #40: Three Drill Defensively

Drill #41: Zig Zag With a Passer—Full Court

Drill #42: Dribble Slap

Drill #43: Two-Ball Pivoting and Dribbling

Drill #44: Dribble, Pass, and Cut

Drill #45: Dribble Tag

Drill #46: Dribble Lay-Up

Chapter 4: Moves 77

Drill #47: Creating Perimeter Space

Drill #48: Three Big Men Post Moves

Drill #49: Two-Line Moves and Shooting

Drill #50: One-Line Offensive Moves

Drill #51: Full-Court Feed the Post

Drill #52: Three Perimeter Moves and Shooting

Drill #53: The Killer Attack

Drill #54: Continuous Moves and Shooting

Drill #55: Perimeter Moves and Screening

Drill #56: Continuous Moves

Drill #57: Individual Perimeter Moves

Drill #58: Individual Post Moves

Chapter 5: Screening 93

Drill #59: Full-Court Screening

Drill #60: Four-Ball Screening and Shooting

Drill #61: Team Continuous Screening

Drill #62: Secondary Break and Screening

Drill #63: Screen-and-Roll Warm-Up

Drill #64: Post Screening and Cutting

Drill #65: Two-Ball Screening, Passing, and Shooting

Drill #66: Reading Screens: Curl or Flair

Drill #67: Reading Screens: Screener or Cutter

Drill #68: Continuous Team Screening

Drill #69: Six Basket Alternating Screens

Drill #70: Continuous Shuffle Screen, Flair Cut Into Dribbling Screen

Drill #71: Buddy Screening

Chapter 6: Cutting 109

Drill #72: Entire Spectrum Cutting

Drill #73: Fast Break and Half-Court Cutting

Drill #74: Six Simultaneous Cutting

Drill #75: Individual All-Purpose

Drill #76: Perimeter and Post Cutting

Drill #77: Warm-Up Cutting

Drill #78: Simulated Half-Court Individual Cutting

Drill #79: Dribble, Pass, Pivot, and Cut

Drill #80: Cutting, Moves, Shooting (Three Players)

Drill #81: Full-Court, Three-Lane Cutting and Passing

Drill #82: Post Open Cuts

Drill #83: Multiple Cutting

Drill #84: Cutters Off Post

Drill #85: Three-Perimeter Cutting and Shooting

Chapter 7: Rebounding 127

Drill #86: Quickness Rebounding

Drill #87: Full-Court Rebounding

Drill #88: Rebounding Agility

Drill #89: Offensive Rebounding Footwork

Drill #90: Block Out and Outlet Pass

Drill #91: Tipping and Conditioning

Drill #92: Scramble Offensive Rebounding

Drill #93: Outlet Pass, Fast Break, and Conditioning

Drill #94: Six-Basket Offensive Rebounding

Drill #95: Rebounding Weave

Drill #96: Competitive Rebounding

Drill #97: Six-Basket Tip and One-on-One

Chapter 8: Warm-Ups 145

Drill #98: Pressure Scoring

Drill #99: Four-Line Dribbling and Shooting

Drill #100: Fundamental Gauntlet

Drill #101: Recovery and Pivoting

Drill #102: Extreme Pressure Lay-Up

Drill #103: Two-Ball Warm-Up and Shooting

Drill #104: Multiple Purpose Warm-Up

Drill #105: Dribbling Moves Warm-Up

Drill #106: Recovery and Break

Drill #107: Half-Court Screening and Cutting

Drill #108: Fly-Pattern Outlet Passes

Drill #109: Heaven or Hell

Chapter 9: Fast Break 161

Drill #110: Multiple Fast-Break Passing
Drill #111: Four-on-Four-on-Four
Drill #112: Three-on-Two-on-One
Drill #113: Three-on-Three-on-Three
Drill #114: Fast Break and Press Breaker
Drill #115: Three-on-Three Call
Drill #116: Three Drill Offensively
Drill #117: Post Fast Break
Drill #118: Three-on-Two to Three-on-Two
Drill #119: Recovery and Transition Circle
Drill #120: Fast-Break Outlet and Baseball Passing
Drill #121: Team Fast Break Into Three-on-Two-on-One
Drill #122: One-on-One Into Five-on-Five
Drill #123: Phases of the Fast Break

Chapter 10: Press Break 179

Drill #124: Full-Speed Passing and Press Breaking
Drill #125: Continuous Passing Out of Traps
Drill #126: Avoid the Flick
Drill #127: Five Drill Defensively
Drill #128: Five Drill Offensively
Drill #129: Three-Versus-Five Press Breaker
Drill #130: Two-Player Posting and Outside Lane Cut
Drill #131: Two-Line Full-Court Beat the Press
Drill #132: Avoid the Herd
Drill #133: Breaking Pressure by Passing and Cutting
Drill #134: Continuous Press Breaker
Drill #135: Phases of the Press Breaker

Chapter 11: Half-Court Offense 197

Drill #136: Recognizing Defenses
Drill #137: Shooting Out of Zone Shell Game
Drill #138: Avoid the Double Down
Drill #139: Combination Passing, Cutting, Screening, and Shooting
Drill #140: Execution of Set Offense
Drill #141: Half-Court Perimeter Offense
Drill #142: Half-Court Post Offense
Drill #143: Five-on-Five Control Scrimmages

About the Author 210

How to Use This Book

This book is all about offensive improvement. The 143 drills included in this book are multi-purposed and dramatically advanced. The veteran coach cannot afford not to have this book; and the rookie coach hopes to be a veteran coach some day.

Each of the 11 chapters has a primary offensive goal, but each of the drills is designed to develop many other fundamentals and team aspects. For example, Chapter 7 is entitled: Rebounding. Rebounding is highlighted in all 12 drills, but shooting, passing, cutting, moves, dribbling, and screening occur in almost all of them. Hence, they are multi-purposed and advanced. To change the drill, just emphasize a different fundamental or team perspective, like shooting. You still get rebounding practice while you are demanding improvement in shooting; and you did not have to reteach a drill format. All drills placed in this chapter could just as easily have been placed in other chapters because of their unrestricted development of other fundamentals and team phases.

As you work on a drill, the player will get the most out of what you emphasize; but each workout will produce practicing on many, many other fundamentals and team facets. For example, conditioning is a part of every drill, as are agility, quickness, and body balance.

While coaching high school basketball, we had the pleasure of playing against many of the top 10 teams in the nation (rated by *USA Today*), and we have played against many NBA players and stars, yet our players never liked to run sprints. We bet yours do not like to run sprints either. An alternative way of getting your players into condition is to run any of the drills in this book. The players will be getting into shape without having to become members of the track team. You also have the added advantage of not wasting time on sprinting without improvement in basketball skills. Each drill is a conditioning drill, an individual basketball improvement drill, and a team strategy lesson.

We realize in modern basketball, players must understand every position on the floor; but we also know it is most difficult to have a power forward become a proficient point guard. Hence, some of the drills develop point guards better than others. Some are designed to foster improvement in the shooting guard or the small forward. Others are aimed primarily at power forwards and post play. Many involve the entire spectrum, from point to post and all in between. Again, what you emphasize is where you will get the most improvement. A section at the beginning of each drill will spell out which position the drill will develop fullest.

A drills finder is the first section in the book. It includes the drill number, drill name, fundamental goals, player positions, the smallest number of players needed to run the drill, and the minimum amount of time required to drill that number of players. With this drills finder, the book becomes an indispensable reference guide. During the busy months of the season, you can quickly find what you want to develop, both by skills and by position, with a quick reference glance to the drills finder. The drills finder and the drill description itself give the reader a perfect cross-reference guide, saving the coach time during the already very cramped and busy basketball season.

Contents of Each Drill

To make the drills easy to understand and implement, every drill will follow the same format. Each drill begins with a number and a name. Following the name will be a position section that lists all of the positions the drill will help to develop. This book will use the typical definition of each position and its classic number:

1. Point guard
2. Shooting guard
3. Small forward
4. Power forward
5. Post

The following section will show the number of players needed to run the drill. This number will always represent the smallest group that must be used. You can add more players, of course, by putting them into a line behind the players mentioned in the drill description. This approach allows the coach to drill a small number of players or the entire team.

The minimum time it takes for all players in the drill to play all positions once is next. You can double the time if you wish for each player to practice each position twice.

The procedure segment comes next and consists of two parts: diagram(s) and step-by-step execution.

The next portion will be the rotation section. Your players will need to know how to rotate from one position to the next within the drill so they can get maximum training at each position. To make the rotation simple, have players go in ascending order of the numbers, offense to defense to end of the line where possible. Some drills do not require a rotation section. In those drills, this section will be eliminated.

The last component is the variation division. Drills can use the same format, and yet teach an entirely different set of fundamentals or team skills. When this variation can be added to a drill, it is fully explained in this grouping.

Drills Finder

		Shooting	Passing	Dribbling	Moves	Screening
#1	Fivo	x	x	x	x	
#2	Crashing the Boards	x	x	x	x	x
#3	Full-Court Shooting Contest	x	x	x	x	
#4	Post Shooting	x	x		x	x
#5	Six-Basket Shooting	x	x	x	x	
#6	Six-Basket Shooting Contest	x	x			
#7	Post Shooting and Conditioning	x	x		x	
#8	Full-Court Golf Shooting Game	x	x			
#9	Six Teams Rotating	x	x	x	x	
#10	Three-Line Shooting Game	x	x			
#11	Individual Reaction Shooting	x	x		x	
#12	Team Three-Point Shooting	x	x			
#13	Pressure Shooting	x		x	x	
#14	Full-Court Shooting and Conditioning	x	x		x	
#15	Speed Shooting	x	x		x	
#16	No-Rim Shooting	x	x			
#17	Team Sprint Passing		x			
#18	Outlet Pass and Shooting	x	x	x	x	
#19	Touch Passing	x	x			
#20	Post Pepper Passing	x	x			
#21	Shooting, Passing, and Touch Passing	x	x			
#22	Passing and Slide Step		x			
#23	Wall Passing		x			
#24	Skip Passing and Shooting	x	x			
#25	Baseball Pass and Dribbling Lay-Up	x	x	x	x	
#26	Fake Passing		x			
#27	Spectrum Passing		x		x	
#28	Diamond Passing		x			
#29	Four-Corner Passing		x			
#30	Two-Player Rapid Fire		x			
#31	Team Post Passing		x			
#32	Two-on-One Passing		x	x		
#33	Combo Overhead and Chest Passing		x			
#34	Pepper Passing		x			
#35	Advanced Dribble Slap	x		x	x	
#36	Full-Court Recovery	x	x	x	x	x
#37	Skip Pass and Penetration	x	x	x	x	
#38	Dribble, Pivot, and Pass Team		x	x	x	
#39	Recovery Lay-Up	x	x	x	x	
#40	Three Defensively	x	x	x	x	x
#41	Zig Zag With a Passer—Full Court		x	x	x	x
#42	Dribble Slap	x		x	x	
#43	Two-Ball Pivoting and Dribbling	x	x	x	x	x
#44	Dribble, Pass, and Cut		x	x	x	
#45	Dribble Tag	x	x	x	x	
#46	Dribble Lay-Up	x	x	x	x	
#47	Creating Perimeter Space	x	x	x	x	

Cutting	Rebounding	Warm-up	Fast break	Pass breaker	Half-court	Point Guard (1)	Shooting Guard (2)	Small Forward (1)	Power Forward (2)	Post (5)	No. of Players	Time (minutes)
x	x	x	x	x		x	x	x			5	12
x	x	x	x		x	x	x	x	x	x	6	8
x	x	x			x	x	x	x	x	x	12	6
x	x	x			x				x	x	6	4
x	x					x	x	x	x	x	12	4
	x	x			x	x	x	x	x	x	12	10
x	x	x			x				x	x	8	4
	x				x	x	x				2	4
x	x	x	x		x	x	x	x	x	x	12	4
	x	x	x			x	x	x	x	x	12	4
x	x	x			x	x	x	x	x	x	12	4
x	x	x	x	x	x	x	x	x			4	6
x	x	x			x	x	x	x			6	4
x	x	x	x	x	x	x	x	x			9	6
x	x	x			x	x	x	x			2	4
	x	x				x	x	x	x	x	2	8
x		x				x	x	x	x	x	4	1
x	x	x	x	x	x	x	x		x	x	8	2
x	x	x			x	x	x	x			4	2
x	x	x	x	x	x	x	x	x	x	x	6	2
x	x	x	x	x	x	x	x	x			3	1
		x				x	x	x	x	x	2	1
x		x				x	x	x	x	x	1	0.5
x	x	x			x	x	x	x	x	x	2	0.5
x	x	x	x	x		x	x	x			3	2
		x			x	x	x	x	x	x	2	1
	x	x	x	x	x	x	x	x	x	x	7	2
		x	x	x	x	x	x	x	x	x	8	2
x		x			x	x	x	x	x	x	8	2
x		x			x	x	x	x	x	x	2	1
x	x	x			x				x	x	8	2
x		x			x	x	x	x	x	x	3	1
x		x	x	x	x	x	x	x	x	x	8	2
		x			x	x	x	x	x	x	6	3
x	x	x	x	x	x	x	x	x	x	x	12	3
x	x	x	x	x	x	x	x	x	x	x	6	2
x	x	x			x	x	x	x	x	x	8	2
x		x	x	x	x	x	x	x			5	1
x	x	x	x	x	x	x	x	x			4	1
x	x	x	x	x		x	x	x			3	2
x		x	x	x	x	x	x	x	x	x	3	2
	x	x	x	x	x	x	x	x	x	x	4	1
x	x	x			x	x	x	x			3	1
x		x	x	x	x	x	x	x			2	1
x	x	x	x	x	x	x	x	x	x	x	10	2
x	x	x	x	x	x	x	x	x	x	x	10	2
x	x	x			x	x	x	x			3	5

		Shooting	Passing	Dribbling	Moves	Screening
#48	Three Big Men Post Moves	x	x	x	x	
#49	Two-Line Moves and Shooting	x	x	x	x	
#50	One-Line Offensive Moves	x		x	x	
#51	Full-Court Feed the Post	x	x	x	x	
#52	Three Perimeter Moves and Shooting	x	x	x	x	x
#53	The Killer Attack	x		x	x	
#54	Continuous Moves and Shooting	x	x	x	x	
#55	Perimeter Moves and Screening	x	x	x	x	x
#56	Continuous Moves	x	x	x	x	
#57	Individual Perimeter Moves	x	x	x	x	x
#58	Individual Post Moves	x	x	x	x	
#59	Full-Court Screening	x	x		x	x
#60	Four-Ball Screening and Shooting	x	x	x	x	x
#61	Team Continuous Screening		x			x
#62	Secondary Break and Screening	x	x	x	x	x
#63	Screen-and-Roll Warm Up	x	x	x		x
#64	Post Screening and Cutting	x	x		x	x
#65	Two Ball Screening, Passing, and Shooting	x	x	x	x	x
#66	Reading Screens Curl or Flair	x	x	x	x	x
#67	Reading Screens Screener or Cutter	x	x	x	x	x
#68	Continuous Team Screening					x
#69	Six Basket Alternating Screens	x	x	x	x	x
#70	Continuous Shuffle Screen, Flair Cut Into Dribbling Screen	x	x	x	x	x
#71	Buddy Screening	x	x	x	x	x
#72	Entire Spectrum Cutting	x	x	x	x	
#73	Fast Break and Half-Court Cutting	x	x	x	x	
#74	Six Simultaneous Cutting	x	x	x	x	x
#75	Individual All-Purpose	x	x	x	x	
#76	Perimeter and Post Cutting	x	x		x	x
#77	Warm-Up Cutting	x	x		x	
#78	Simulated Half-Court Individual Cutting				x	x
#79	Dribble, Pass, Pivot, and Cut		x	x	x	x
#80	Cutting, Moves, Shooting (Three Players)	x	x	x	x	x
#81	Full-Court Three-Lane Cutting and Passing		x	x	x	
#82	Post Open Cuts	x	x	x	x	x
#83	Multiple Cutting					
#84	Cutters Off Post	x	x	x	x	x
#85	Three-Perimeter Cutting and Shooting	x	x	x	x	
#86	Quickness Rebounding	x	x	x	x	
#87	Full-Court Rebounding	x	x	x	x	
#88	Rebounding Agility	x	x	x	x	x
#89	Offensive Rebounding Footwork	x		x	x	
#90	Block Out and Outlet Pass	x	x	x	x	x
#91	Tipping and Conditioning		x	x	x	
#92	Scramble Offensive Rebounding	x	x	x	x	
#93	Outlet Pass, Fast Break, and Conditioning	x	x	x	x	
#94	Six-Basket Offensive Rebounding	x	x	x	x	x

Cutting	Rebounding	Warm-up	Fast break	Pass breaker	Half-court	Point Guard (1)	Shooting Guard (2)	Small Forward (1)	Power Forward (2)	Post (5)	No. of Players	Time (minutes)
x	x	x			x				x	x	3	5
x	x	x			x	x	x	x			4	4
	x	x			x	x	x	x			1	3
x	x	x	x	x	x	x	x	x	x	x	6	3
x	x	x			x	x	x	x			3	2
x	x	x	x	x	x	x	x	x			4	3
x	x	x			x	x	x	x			3	5
x		x			x	x	x	x			3	5
x	x	x			x	x	x	x			3	5
x	x	x			x	x	x	x			2	5
x	x	x			x				x	x	4	5
x	x	x	x		x	x	x	x	x	x	6	3
x	x	x			x	x	x	x	x	x	6	5
x		x			x	x	x	x	x	x	3	1
x	x	x	x	x	x	x	x	x	x	x	11	3
x	x	x			x	x	x	x			4	1
x		x			x				x	x	7	1
x	x	x			x	x	x	x	x	x	8	2
x	x	x			x	x	x	x	x	x	7	2
x	x	x			x	x	x	x			5	3
x		x			x	x	x	x	x	x	9	1
x	x	x			x	x	x	x	x	x	12	2
x	x	x			x	x	x	x	x	x	3	1
x	x	x	x		x	x	x	x	x	x	2	3
x	x	x	x	x	x	x	x	x	x	x	12	3
x	x		x		x	x	x	x			6	2
x	x	x			x	x	x	x	x	x	2	3
x	x	x			x	x	x	x			2	1
x	x	x	x		x	x	x	x	x	x	4	2
x	x	x			x	x	x	x			4	2
x		x			x	x	x	x			1	0.5
x		x	x	x	x	x	x	x			3	1
x	x	x			x	x	x	x			3	3
x		x	x	x		x	x	x			3	1
x	x	x	x		x				x	x	7	5
x		x	x	x	x	x	x	x			4	2
x	x	x			x	x	x	x	x	x	2	2
x	x	x			x	x	x	x			3	3
x	x	x			x	x	x	x	x	x	6	3
x	x	x			x	x	x	x	x	x	8	3
x	x	x			x	x	x	x			4	2
	x	x			x	x	x	x	x	x	2	2
x	x	x	x		x	x	x	x	x	x	13	4
x	x	x		x	x	x	x	x	x	x	12	2
x	x	x			x	x	x	x	x	x	9	3
x	x	x	x		x	x	x	x	x	x	7	3
x	x	x	x		x	x	x	x	x	x	18	2

		Shooting	Passing	Dribbling	Moves	Screening
#95	Rebounding Weave					
#96	Competitive Rebounding	x	x	x	x	
#97	Six-Basket Tip and One-on-One	x		x	x	
#98	Pressure Scoring	x	x	x	x	
#99	Four-Line Dribbling and Shooting	x	x		x	
#100	Fundamental Gauntlet	x	x	x	x	x
#101	Recovery and Pivoting	x	x	x	x	x
#102	Extreme Pressure Lay-Up	x	x	x	x	
#103	Two-Ball Warm-Up and Shooting	x	x	x	x	
#104	Multiple Purpose Warm-Up	x	x	x	x	x
#105	Dribbling Moves Warm-Up	x	x	x	x	
#106	Recovery and Break	x	x	x	x	x
#107	Half-Court Screening and Cutting	x	x	x	x	x
#108	Fly-Pattern Outlet Pass	x	x	x	x	
#109	Heaven or Hell	x	x	x	x	
#110	Multiple Fast-Break Passing	x	x	x	x	
#111	Four-on-Four-on-Four	x	x	x	x	
#112	Three-on-Two-on-One	x	x	x	x	
#113	Three-on-Three-on-Three	x	x	x	x	
#114	Fast Break and Press Breaker	x	x	x	x	
#115	Three-on-Three Call	x	x	x	x	
#116	Three Offensively	x	x	x		
#117	Post Fast Break	x	x	x	x	
#118	Three-on-Two to Three-on-Two	x	x	x		
#119	Recovery and Transition Circle	x	x	x		x
#120	Fast-Break Outlet and Baseball Passing	x	x	x	x	
#121	Team Fast Break Into Three-on-Two-on-One	x	x	x	x	
#122	One-on-One Into Five-on-Five	x	x	x	x	x
#123	Phases of the Fast Break	x	x	x	x	x
#124	Full-Speed Passing and Press Breaking	x	x	x	x	
#125	Continuous Passing Out of Traps		x	x		
#126	Avoid the Flick	x		x	x	
#127	Five Defensively	x	x	x	x	
#128	Five Offensively	x	x	x	x	x
#129	Three-Versus-Five Press Breaker	x	x	x	x	x
#130	Two-Player Posting and Outside Lane Cut	x	x		x	
#131	Two-Line Full-Court Beat the Press	x	x	x	x	
#132	Avoid the Herd			x	x	
#133	Breaking Pressure by Passing and Cutting	x	x	x	x	
#134	Continuous Press Breaker	x	x	x	x	
#135	Phases of the Press Breaker		x	x	x	
#136	Recognizing Defenses	x	x	x	x	x
#137	Shooting Out of Zone Shell Game	x	x	x	x	x
#138	Avoid the Double Down	x	x	x	x	
#139	Combination Passing, Cutting, Screening, and Shooting	x	x	x	x	x
#140	Execution of Set Offense	x	x	x	x	x
#141	Half-Court Perimeter Offense	x	x	x	x	x
#142	Half-Court Post Offense	x	x	x	x	x
#143	Five-on-Five Control Scrimmages	x	x	x	x	x

Cutting	Rebounding	Warm-up	Fast break	Pass breaker	Half-court	Point Guard (1)	Shooting Guard (2)	Small Forward (1)	Power Forward (2)	Post (5)	No. of Players	Time (minutes)
	x	x			x	x	x	x	x	x	3	0.5
x	x	x			x	x	x	x	x	x	4	3
x	x	x			x	x	x	x	x	x	12	6
x	x	x			x	x	x	x	x	x	4	2
x	x	x	x		x	x	x	x	x	x	8	2
x	x	x	x	x	x	x	x	x	x	x	10	2
x	x	x	x	x	x	x	x	x	x	x	2	1
x	x	x	x		x	x	x	x			3	1.5
x	x	x	x		x	x	x	x	x	x	8	4
x	x	x	x	x	x	x	x	x	x	x	5	2
x	x	x			x	x	x	x			2	1
x	x	x	x	x	x	x	x	x	x	x	4	2
x	x	x			x	x	x	x	x	x	12	2
x	x	x	x	x		x	x	x	x	x	4	2
x	x	x	x	x		x	x	x	x	x	2	2
x	x	x	x			x	x	x	x	x	6	3
x	x	x	x			x	x	x	x	x	12	5
x	x	x	x			x	x	x	x	x	5	2
x	x	x	x			x	x	x	x	x	9	4
x	x	x	x	x		x	x	x	x	x	8	6
x	x	x	x	x		x	x	x	x	x	6	4
x	x	x	x	x		x	x	x			3	3
x	x	x							x	x	5	5
x	x	x				x	x	x			7	4
x	x	x				x	x	x	x	x	10	1
x	x	x				x	x	x	x	x	3	2
x	x	x	x	x		x	x	x	x	x	5	2
x	x	x	x	x	x	x	x	x	x	x	10	10
x	x	x	x			x	x	x	x	x	12	4
x	x	x		x		x	x	x	x	x	12	4
x		x		x	x	x	x	x	x	x	6	2
	x	x	x	x	x	x	x	x			2	1
x		x	x	x	x	x	x	x	x	x	5	3
x	x	x	x	x	x	x	x	x	x	x	5	3
x	x	x	x	x	x	x	x	x	x	x	8	5
x	x	x	x	x		x	x	x	x	x	4	2
x	x	x	x	x	x	x	x	x	x	x	9	3
		x		x	x	x	x	x			3	1.5
x	x	x	x	x	x	x	x	x	x	x	4	2
x	x	x	x	x	x	x	x	x	x	x	8	4
x		x	x	x		x	x	x	x	x	11	4
x	x	x			x	x	x	x	x	x	10	6
x	x	x			x	x	x	x	x	x	7	3
x	x	x	x	x	x	x	x	x	x	x	6	4
x	x	x	x	x	x	x	x	x	x	x	4	3
x	x	x			x	x	x	x	x	x	5	5
x	x	x			x	x	x	x			8	9
x	x	x			x				x	x	7	8
x	x	x	x	x	x	x	x	x	x	x	10	10

Two Drills to Illustrate

Because the drills are given in each chapter without explanation as to how to teach individual or team skills, this section will offer two drills (one individual and one team) to help you understand how you can adjust the drill to incorporate almost any fundamental or team concept you wish. It would take several volumes to explain such detail for each drill presented in the following chapters. But with these two, the Fivo drill (Drill #1) and the crashing-the-boards drill (Drill #2), you will see how you can add to and subtract from all the drills to get maximum benefits from this book. Since this volume is truly an advanced, multi-purpose, offensive drills book, these two drills will be presented in the same format as all the drills. Explanations of future possible creations by you will be added in *italicized* form. You can change all the drills to comply exactly to your specific offensive system.

After explaining these two drills and illustrating several options you can create to comply exactly with your own offensive system, the other drills will be left as they are for you to make your own creations.

Another great benefit your players will derive from the drills: improved basketball IQs. Team facets occur in the same order in the drills as they would happen in a game, whether you are drilling for individual advancement or team betterment. In the Fivo drill, the perimeter three—especially the point guard—will face the situations presented in the drill many times during any game, and in exactly the same sequence. In the crashing the board drill, your team will run your half-court offense, miss the shot, get the offensive rebound, score, hustle back on defense, recover a loose ball, fast break, secondary break, into team offense. That pattern is exactly what occurs every game you play, and in that same order.

Drill #1: Fivo

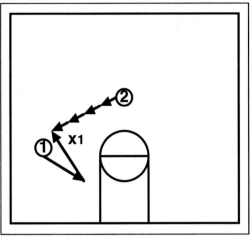

Diagram 0-1

Diagram 0-2

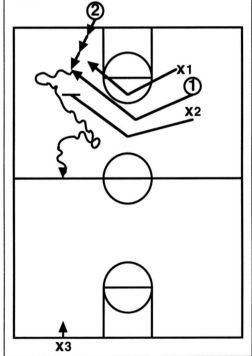

Diagram 0-3

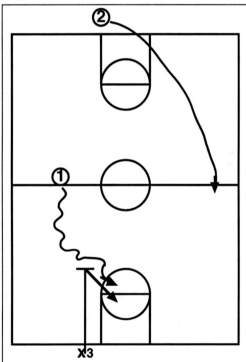

Diagram 0-4

Positions: 1, 2, 3
Number of Players: 5
Time: 12 minutes

Description:

This drill has five parts. In step one (Diagram 0-1), 1 uses a V-cut to free himself from X1. As soon as 1 catches the ball, 1 squares up to the basket, and then passes back to 2. 1 again tries to free himself. Repeat five times before going to step two.

In step two (Diagram 0-2), 1 goes one-on-one against X1 in an attempt to score. 1 should not take a bad shot. If X1 prevents the good shot, 1 can pass back to 2, then 1 gets open again, and goes one-on-one against X1. Repeat five times before going to step three. Steps one and two can be combined if you wish. *You can even alter the drill to allow 1 to go inside and post-up X1 after passing back to 2. You would want to do the drill in this way if posting a wing player is part of your offensive system.* 1 must score three of the five times, or he cannot advance to step three. After mid-season, 1 must win four of the five battles before moving on to step three.

In step three, 2 takes the ball out of bounds and attempts to get it inbounds to 1 as he tries to shake X1 from a face-guard defense, which is attempted five times. It must be successful three of the five times, or 1 cannot advance to step four. From mid-season, 1 must win four of the five battles.

In step four (Diagram 0-3), X2 joins X1 to try to keep 1 from receiving the inbounds pass from 2. X1 and X2 may double-team 1 in any manner, X1 face guard and X2 play behind, or X1 play the left side and X2 the right, for example. Once the ball is inbounded to 1, 1 must dribble the ball across half-court against double-team pressure of X1 and X2. 1 must be successful three out of five times before advancing to step five. *2 can step inbounds, and once 1 picks up his dribble, 2 can become an outlet pass; but 1 must get open again for a pass from 2.* 1 must learn to keep the dribble alive—even against double-team pressure.

In step five (Diagram 0-4), X1 and X2 drop off at mid-court, and 1 dribble-drives hard for a lay-up by outmaneuvering X3 who has entered the court from the other baseline. 1 must win this battle three out of five times; otherwise, 1 must begin the entire process all over again. Step five can be combined with step four to speed up the process. *If you would like to drill on a two-on-one fast break, simply allow 2 to continue down the floor and he becomes the second offensive player against X3. Or you could demand that 2 go to the baseline then flash pivot back up against X3 into a post position. 1 must dribble and find the perfect entry pass position to 2.* As you can see, the alternatives to include in any phase of your offensive system are unlimited, which is true throughout this drill book. Your drills will have infinite possibilities.

Rotations: 1 to 2 to X1 to X2 to X3 to 1.

Drill #2: Crashing the Boards

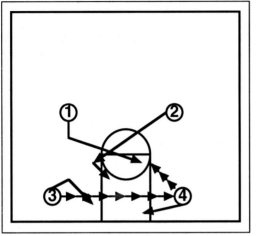

Diagram 0-5

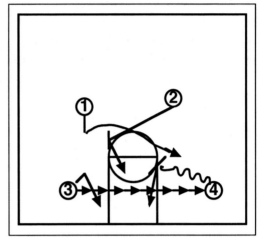

Diagram 0-6

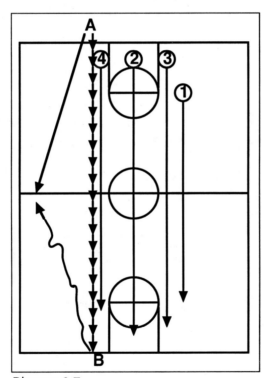

Diagram 0-7

Positions: 1, 2, 3, 4, 5
Number of Players: 6
Time: 8 minutes

Description:

As shown in Diagram 0-5, 1, 2, 3, and 4 pass the ball around the horn until 3 passes to 4 or 4 passes to 3. This pass signals 1 and 2 to cross cut. *Or if you have a guard-to-guard screen in your offensive system, you could use it here.* 1 shoots the ball while 2, 3, and 4 crash the offensive boards for the rebound. When the shot is missed, the rebounder can tip or rebound the ball and return to the floor, then pump fake, and shoot the power lay-up.

Diagram 0-6 displays a screening maneuver to set up the shot. 4 received the pass from 3 and dribbled toward the neck of the key. Meanwhile, 2 has set a screen for 1. 1 should dip and set his imaginary defender up for the screen. 1 continues off of 4's screen. 1 takes the handoff and shoots the jump shot as 2, 3, and 4 crash the offensive boards. *If you are stressing an inside game in your offensive system, you may devise it here, use it to obtain the shot, then continue with the drill.*

Once the shot is made, the ball is tipped to A (Diagram 0-7). A immediately throws the baseball pass to B, who is out of bounds on the other end of the court. 1, 2, 3, and 4 must convert to defense and race to the other end of the court before B can receive the ball and drive for a lay up. A follows his baseball pass to mid-court so he can be ready for the final phase of the drill.

If B cannot get an open shot, B rolls the ball to A who passes to 1 and 2, 3, 4, and A fill the lanes on a fast-break return to the original basket. *If you run a form fast break or a numbers break, you could practice it here. If you also have a secondary break before getting into your offense, this spot is perfect for it.*

Rotations: 1 to 2 to 3 to 4 to A to B to 1

As you can see, the drills are not complex; but they are advanced. They are also multi-purposed, *and you can add or subtract at any level to include your own offensive scheme.*

You do not need to teach a lot of the drills. Six or eight will do for any given year. But you need for the drills to fit your personnel—which will change from year to year. And you will likely find two or three you had overlooked that might really help immensely toward the most important time of the season: tournament time.

1

Shooting

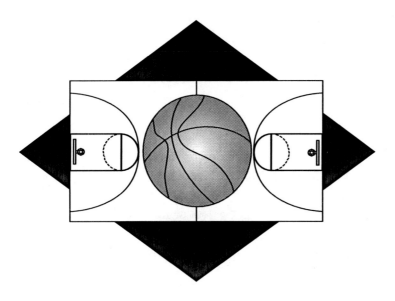

Drill #3: Full-Court Shooting Contest

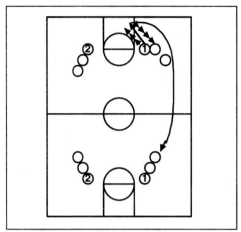

Diagram 1-1

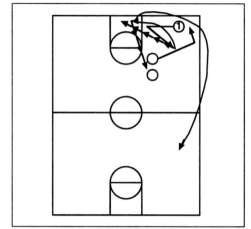

Diagram 1-2

Positions: 1, 2, 3, 4, 5
Number of Players: 12
Time: 6 minutes

Description:
- Place two sets of teams as shown in Diagram 1-1. Three players in each line. Front player in each line has a basketball.
- On command, all four players shoot the ball. Each gets the rebound, whether made or missed. The player passes to the next player in line. The coach can require outlet pass, chest pass, and so forth.
- Player then sprints down the floor to the end of the line where his teammates are. So Diagram 1-1 will not be cluttered, only the movement of player 1 is shown.
- Put six minutes on the clock and keep score. Team leading at the end of six minutes wins. The other team pays a penalty determined by the margin of the loss.

Variations:
- Diagram 1-2 illustrates an option you may wish to use. Place four cones on the court. Each potential shooter runs a V-cut around the cone, receives a pass from the first player in line, shoots, then rebounds and passes to next player in line. The first player in line would have assumed the new cutting position. The shooter-rebounder-outlet passer sprints to the line at the other end of the court.
- A second variation is to have players make a move before shooting. It can be a dribbling move: reverse or spin, or it can be part of the rocker step (jab step, jab step-retreat, etc.).

Rotations: Have teams exchange sides of the court and go again.

Drill #4: Post Shooting

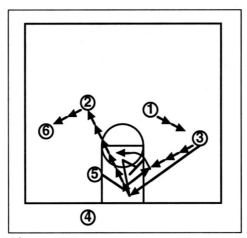

Diagram 1-3

Positions: 4, 5
Number of Players: 6
Time: 4 minutes

Description:
- Line players up as shown in Diagram 1-3. One sequence of the procedure will be discussed. All other series will follow this chain of occurrence.
- 1 passes to 3. 5 flash pivots. 3 passes to 5. 5 pivots and shoots. You could require 5 to make an offensive move before shooting. You could demand that 5 gets the rebound if he misses the shot, pump fakes, and then scores a power lay-up.
- To continue the sequence: 3 rebounds and outlet passes to 2.
- 1 replaces 3's vacated spot.
- 5 slides down the lane while 3 sets a screen for 5.
- 5 uses 3's screen and cuts to side post for a pass and another shot. 3 replaces 1's vacated spot.
- 2 passes to 6, and 6 passes to 5 who pivots (or makes a move) and shoots.
- 6 rebounds while 2 fills 6's spot. 6 passes to 3 who has replaced 1. 6 sets a screen for 5, or you can stipulate for 5 to flash pivot.
- 5 continues in this movement for two minutes before 4 and 5 exchange places.

Rotations:
- 1 to 3, 3 to 1, 2 to 6, 6 to 2
- After two minutes, 4 to 5 and 5 to 4

Drill #5: Six-Basket Shooting

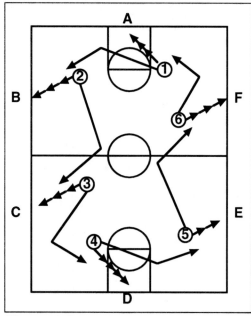

Diagram 1-4

Positions: 1, 2, 3, 4, 5
Number of Players: 12
Time: 4 minutes

Description:
- Line players up as shown in Diagram 1-4. Six teams of two. Each team has a basket.
- A, B, C, D, E, and F rebound, pass, and defend.
- 1, 2, 3, 4, 5, and 6 shoot the jump shot, and then move on to the next basket running a V-cut.
- Example: 1 shoots at basket. A rebounds. Meanwhile, B has rebounded 2's shot. 1 breaks hard toward B's basket. B passes to 1, who shoots his jump shot. This process continues around the six baskets for two minutes before the shooters rotate to rebounders, and the rebounders rotate to shooters.

Variations:
- Instead of just shooting, cutting, and receiving a pass at the next basket for another jump shot, the rebounder at that new basket passes the ball, moves out, and defends the shooter, compelling an offensive move off the dribble.

- Instead of just shooting, cutting, receiving a pass, and going one-on-one with the rebounder-defender, the two can go after the rebound (making this drill also a rebounding drill).
- The shooter shoots then moves quickly to the next basket, where he receives an outlet pass from the basket where he just attempted a shot.
- Make it a zone shooting drill. The shooter receives a pass from the next basket, pump fakes a shot, then dribbles one dribble or two dribbles to one side or the other, and shoots a three-point attempt.

Rotations:
- A to 1, 1 to A
- B to 2, 2 to B
- C to 3, 3 to C
- D to 4, 4 to D
- E to 5, 5 to E
- F to 6, 6 to F

Drill #6: Six-Basket Shooting Contest

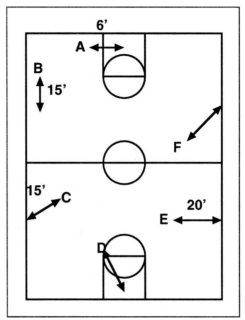

Diagram 1-5

Positions: 1, 2, 3, 4, 5
Number of Players: 12
Time: 10 minutes

Description:
- Six players begin as shooters, and six as rebounders.
- Each shooter must make the shot at his basket before he can sprint to the next basket.
- Spots at the six baskets are:
    ✓ Short corner six feet from the basket.
    ✓ Corner shot 15 feet from basket (or three-point shot, if you desire).
    ✓ 15-foot bank shot from 45-degree angle.
    ✓ Corner (neck) of the free-throw lane.
    ✓ Head of key at the three-point arc.
    ✓ 45-degree angle from the three-point arc.
- Six teams of two (one rebounder and one shooter) are operating at the same time.
- Shooter can go once around or twice around before rotating with his rebounder.

- Instead of competing against a teammate, shooter can be required to go against the clock. Ten times around in five minutes is a good shooting session. Remember: shots must be made before the player can move on to the next basket.

Variations:
- Divide squad into two teams. Have all members of the team begin at spot A. Turn the clock on. Stop the clock when all team members have circled the court and make the shot back at spot A. Team that has the lowest time on the clock wins.
- Designate one spot, like D, that must be made on the first attempt or the shooter has to go back to the beginning basket. This spot can be changed from day to day.

Rotations: Shooter to rebounder, and rebounder to shooter

Drill #7: Post Shooting and Conditioning

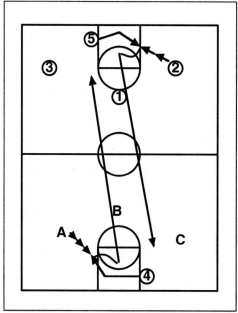

Diagram 1-6

Positions: 4, 5
Number of Players: 8
Time: 4 minutes (early season)/10 minutes (late season)

Description:
- Line up six perimeter players, each with a basketball (three on each end of the court). Have one post player in the lane on each end of the court.
- Post player (5 in Diagram 1-6) cuts, gives the perimeter player of his choice an open hand signal, receives the pass, turns (or makes a move) and shoots. 5 then sprints to the other end of the court (4 is doing the same thing at the other end of the court).
- The manager returns the ball to the perimeter passer (2 in Diagram 1-6).
- 5 now makes a cut to a perimeter player at the opposite end of the court, receives a pass, turns, and shoots. 5 again sprints back to his original end of the court.
- This process continues for two minutes early in the season. Work up to five minutes by the end of the season.
- Perimeter players should be working on their entry pass (flip pass, for example) while post players are working on their moves and shooting.

Variations:

- You can add a post defender and make it a competitive game. Whenever a post player is stopped twice consecutively, the post defender becomes the attacker and the attacker becomes the defender. The defender races the length of the court with his attacker.
- Require the racing post attacker to rebound a missed shot before he begins his cut for shooting. In the diagram, after the manager has passes the ball back to 2, 2 shoots. 4 would have to be really hustling to get to 2's end of the court. 5 would be hustling down the other side of the court. 4 rebounds 2's shot. 4 can tip, or 4 can bring the rebound down, pump fake, and shoot a power lay-up. 4 then flash pivots toward a perimeter player, and the drill continues.

Drill #8: Full-Court Golf Shooting Game

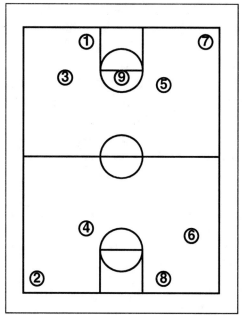

Diagram 1-7

Positions: 1, 2, 3
Number of Players: 2
Time: 4 minutes

Description:
- Mark off the nine spots shown in Diagram 1-7.
- Two players compete. One shooter and one rebounder-passer. After the shooter completes his round, the two exchange places.
- One player shoots until he makes the shot from each spot. If it takes two shots to make it, the player scores par. If he makes it on the first attempt, score one under par. If on the third shot, one over par, and so forth.
- Once a player makes the shot, he sprints down the floor to the other end and shoots from the next spot (notice all odd spots are on one end and all even on the other). The rebounder-passer must also sprint.
- Shooter has two minutes to compete the course. Anything after two minutes, a stroke-per-hole penalty is charged for playing too slow.

Rotations: After two minutes, the rebounder-passer becomes the shooter and the shooter becomes the rebounder-passer.

Drill #9: Six Teams Rotating

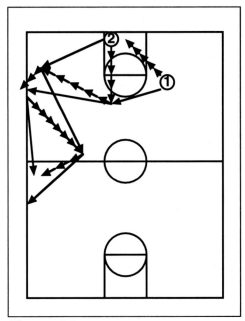

Diagram 1-8

Positions: 1, 2, 3, 4, 5
Number of Players: 12
Time: 4 minutes

Description:
- Put two players at each basket. (Only one group is shown in Diagram 1-8 to eliminate a crowded court for explanations).
- 1 shoots and 2 rebounds.
- 2 outlet passes to 1, and then 2 sprints to get a pass from 1 for a jump shot.
- 2 shoots and 1 rebounds.
- The drill continues in this fashion around the six baskets.
- Go in one direction one day and the other direction the next.

Variations:
- Have the rebounder blast out with the rebound before passing.
- Have the shooter make a dribbling move before shooting.
- Have any missed shot rebounded, followed by a power lay-up.
- Have the shooter make a cut before receiving a pass. Then the shooter can shoot off the cut or make a move off the cut.

Drill #10: Three-Line Shooting Game

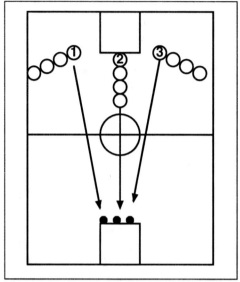

Diagram 1-9

Positions: 1, 2, 3, 4, 5
Number of Players: 12
Time: 4 minutes

Description:

- Divide twelve-player squad into three groups as shown in Diagram 1-9.
- On the coach's signal, first player in each line shoots. Each line is 15 feet from the basket.
- Player who shoots races in to get his rebound (made or missed). If player gets this rebound before it hits the floor, player can shoot a second shot.
- If player does not get rebound before it hits floor, player cannot shoot a second shot.
- Player, after shooting either the first or the second shot, rebounds and passes to next player in line.
- After the pass, player races to other end of the court and shoots a free throw. He retrieves the ball and places it back at the free-throw line. Each shooting line has a ball at the opposite free-throw line.
- Score goes to 50. First shot is worth three points, second shot is worth two points, and the free throw is worth one point.

Rotations: Rotate the lines from 1 to 2 to 3 to 1, so shots will come from all angles.

Drill #11: Individual Reaction Shooting

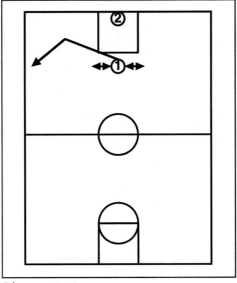

Diagram 1-10

Positions: 1, 2, 3, 4, 5
Number of Players: 12
Time: 4 minutes

Description:
- Divide squad into pairs. Each pair has a basketball. Use six baskets.
- 1 slides backward and forward without looking at 2. 2 yells, "Ball," as he rolls ball two or three steps away from 1.
- 1 turns as he hears, "Ball." 1 recovers ball and shoots. 2 rebounds.
- 1 follows his shot, touches the baseline, sprints back to the foul line, and begins his sliding again. This process should continue for about two minutes before the players exchange spots.

Variations:
- After 1 shoots and scores, 1 executes a cut to the next basket where he will try to tap the board without the player stationed in that position being able to block 1 out. Then 1 moves out to the free-throw line and begins the procedure again.
- Instead of following his shot and touching the baseline, 1 follows his shot while 2 tries to box him off of the boards.
- 2 rolls ball and yells, "Ball." 2 follows the roll and plays one-on-one defense against 1.

Rotations: 1 to 2, 2 to 1

Drill #12: Team Three-Point Shooting

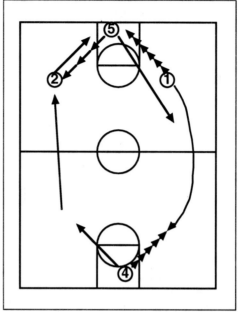

Diagram 1-11

Positions: 1, 2, 3
Number of Players: 4
Time: 6 minutes

Description:
- 1 shoots and sprints to opposite end of the court.
- 5 rebounds and passes to 2 who sprinted from opposite end. 5 sprints to the opposite end of the court for a shot.
- 4 passes to 1 who shoots.
- 2 follows his own shot and becomes the new 5.
- After passing to 1, 4 sprints to opposite end of court.
- 2 passes to 4, who shoots and follows his own shot.
- 1 follows his shot and passes to the sprinting 5.

Variation:
- To simulate faking a defender who is closing out on the shot, shooters can fake a three-point shot, pull the ball down, dribble to one side with one dribble, and shoot a three-point shot.

Drill #13: Pressure Shooting

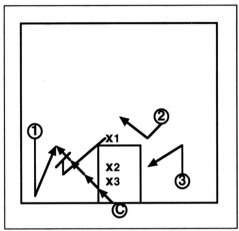

Diagram 1-12

Positions: 1, 2, 3
Number of Players: 6
Time: 4 minutes

Description:
- X1, X2, and X3 face the coach.
- Coach tosses ball to either 1, 2, or 3. Meanwhile 1, 2, and 3 have been making cuts.
- In Diagram 1-12, coach tosses ball to 1. X1 closes out on 1. 1 has option to shoot or drive by X1. 1 can shoot after his dribble penetration or pass ball to 2 or 3. X2 must decide to stop the dribble penetration, and X3 must close out on the new pass receiver-shooter.
- X3 rebounds the shot, gives the ball to the coach, and the drill continues.
- Coach can require the player who receives the first pass to shoot. Doing so simulates shooting against zone coverage.
- Coach can demand shooter to follow his own shot and get the offensive rebound, or all attackers can crash the boards while all defenders block out.

Rotations: After two minutes, offense becomes defense and defense becomes offense.

Drill #14: Full-Court Shooting and Conditioning

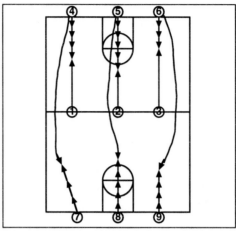

Diagram 1-13

Positions: 1, 2, 3
Number of Players: 9
Time: 6 minutes

Description:
- Line players up as shown in Diagram 1-13.
- Players 1, 2, and 3 sprint toward players 4, 5, and 6.
- Players 4, 5, and 6 pass to players 1, 2, and 3. 1, 2, and 3 take jump shots and crash the offensive boards.
- As soon as 4, 5, and 6 have passed the ball, they sprint to the opposite end of the court where they receive a pass from 7, 8, and 9. 4, 5, and 6 jump shoot and crash the offensive boards.
- The drill continues in this way for six minutes.

Variations:
- Instead of 4, 5, and 6 sprinting to the other end of the court after they have passed the ball, they block out on 1, 2, and 3's crashing of the offensive boards. Then 4, 5, and 6 sprint to other end of court. Drill continues in this fashion.
- Instead of 1, 2, and 3 shooting an immediate jump shot, 1, 2, and 3 make a predetermined offensive move (either off rocker step or off the dribble) before they shoot.
- Instead of a direct sprint down the floor, the sprinters can run a cut before receiving the ball.
- Any combination of the previous three variations can be run.

Drill #15: Speed Shooting

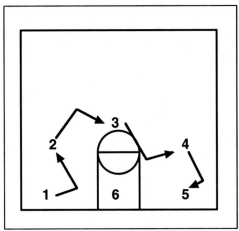

Diagram 1-14

Positions: 1, 2, 3
Number of Players: 2
Time: 4 minutes (for all 100 shots)

Description:
- Teammates pair up in groups of two.
- 1, 2, 3, 4, and 5 show the shooting spots. 6 is the rebound spot.
- 6 passes to 1 and 1 shoots. 1 then cuts and moves quickly to spot 2 while 6 rebounds. 6 passes quickly to spot 2, who must shoot quickly.
- 6 rebounds while the shooter moves from spot 2 to spot 3 with a predetermined cut. 6 passes to spot 3 where a quick shot is taken.
- This pattern continues around the court and back, giving the shooter 10 shots before the players exchange responsibilities.
- Scores may be kept during the entire practice to see who is the best shooter. Spots may be changed from day to day to get shooting practice from your offensive spots.
- You should run a rigorous drill, and then go quickly to this shooting drill five times during practice. Each player shoots 30 times on the first run of the drill, 20 times on the next three runs, and 10 times on the last run, giving each shooter 100 shots during practice.

Variations:
- Require a move by the shooter before shooting, but the move must be made quickly.
- Require the rebounder to rebound a missed shot, pump fake, and then score a power lay-up.
- Combine any of these variations with the regular drill.

Drill #16: No-Rim Shooting

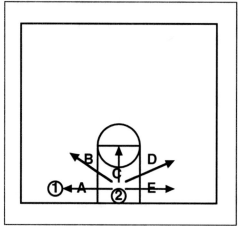

Diagram 1-15

Positions: 1, 2, 3, 4, 5
Number of Players: 2
Time: 8 minutes

Description:
- 1 shoots and 2 rebounds.
- 1 shoots from six feet until he makes it without the ball touching the rim. Then 1 moves back to nine feet and he shoots until he makes it without the ball touching the rim. Then he shoots from 12 feet. 2 rebounds each shot and passes to 1.
- After 1 has made the three shots in line A, 1 and 2 exchange duties.
- The process is repeated in line B, and then lines C, D, and E.

Variation:
- Let each player shoot for one minute and see who gets the farthest. Starting from where each got, begin another one-minute shooting duration. See where each player gets. Repeat this drill for four minutes with each shooter.

2

Passing

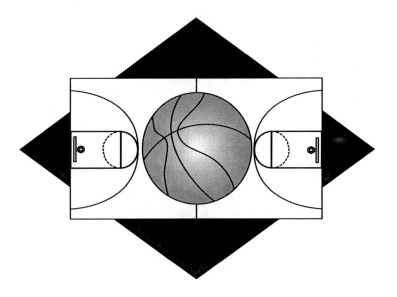

Drill #17: Team Sprint Passing

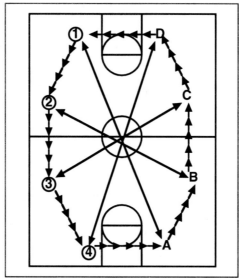

Diagram 2-1

Positions: 1, 2, 3, 4, 5
Number of Players: 4
Time: 1 minute

Description:
- Line players up at 1, 2, 3, and 4 as shown in Diagram 2-1.
- 1 passes to 2, who passes to 3, who passes to 4, who passes to 1, and so on.
- After each player passes the ball, he sprints to a new location. 1 sprints to position A. 2 dashes to B. 3 runs to C, and 4 races to D. After the next pass, each player runs back to his original location. The players continue alternating locations after each pass.
- Passing continues around the court until four passes have been practiced going left and going right.
- Coach can require two or three rounds instead of one round of four passes both left and right (eight passes).
- Coach can require specific cuts as players sprint from one passing position to the next. V-cut once. Backdoor cut next, and so forth.

Variations:
- Add a fifth player by positioning players differently.
- Make the sprinting distance shorter and require quicker passes.
- Require fake passes before making the actual pass.

Drill #18: Outlet Pass and Shooting

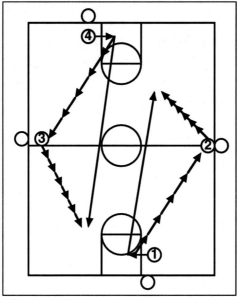

Diagram 2-2

Positions: 1, 4, 5
Number of Players: 8
Time: 2 minutes

Description:
- Place players as shown in Diagram 2-2. Have a minimum of two players in each line.
- 1 outlet passes to 2. 1 sprints straight down the floor while 2 pivots to face the other goal.
- 2 passes to 1 (overhead flip). 1 moves to any spot on the right side of the floor for a jump shot.
- 4 rebounds 1's shot, made or missed, and outlet passes to 3. 4 sprints straight down the floor.
- 1 goes to the end of 4's line, and 4 goes to the end of 1's line.
- The drill continues for two minutes before rotation occurs.
- Two balls should be used: one ball with 1, and one ball with 4.

Variations:
- Instead of an outlet pass, let the rebounder blast out with a dribble or two before making the outlet pass.

- Instead of a jump shot, have player shoot a contested lay-up (contested by the rebounder).
- Instead of a jump shot, have player make a dribbling move before shooting the jump shot.
- Instead of shooting the jump shot, have 4 set a screen for 1 and 1 set a screen for 4. After the screen, the screener rolls to get the rebound off of the jump shot.

Rotations: 1 to 2, and 2 to 1. 3 to 4, and 4 to 3.

Drill #19: Touch Passing

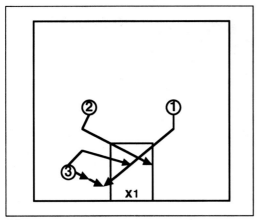

Diagram 2-3

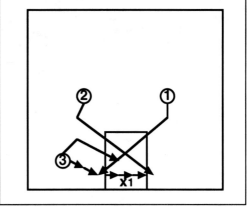

Diagram 2-4

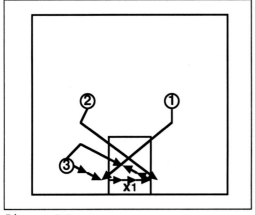

Diagram 2-5

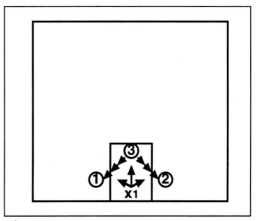

Diagram 2-6

Positions: 1, 2, 3
Number of Players: 4
Time: 2 minutes

Description:
- This drill has five phases. In the first phase (Diagram 2-3), 1 gets a lay-up. 1 passes to 2, who passes to 3, who touch passes to 1 for the lay-up.
- In the second phase (Diagram 2-4), 2 gets the lay-up. Players follow the same touch passing as in the first phase. Then 1 touch passes to 2, who has cut to the basket for the lay-up.

- In the third phase (Diagram 2-5), 3 gets the jump shot. Players follow the same touch passing as in the second phase. Instead of 2 shooting a lay-up, 2 touch passes to 3, who shoots the jump shot.
- In the fourth phase (Diagram 2-6), players follow the same touch passing as in the third phase. 3 now has the ball, but 3 does not shoot the jump shot. Instead 3 touch passes to either 2 or 1 for the lay-up.
- In the fifth phase, X1 steps out to defend the touch passing of 1, 2, and 3 inside. This move compels those attackers to make quick decisions.
- At each phase of the drill, when a shot is taken, all players crash the offensive boards for either a tip or a rebound and a power lay-up after pump fakes.

Rotations: 1 to 2 to 3 to X1 to 1

Drill #20: Post Pepper Passing

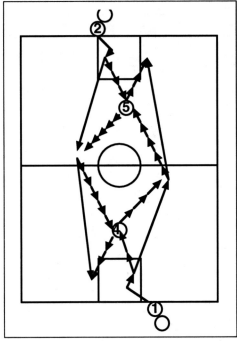

Diagram 2-7

Positions: 1, 2, 3, 4, 5
Number of Players: 6
Time: 2 minutes

Description:
- 1 passes to 4, and 1 begins sprinting.
- 4 passes to 1 on the sprint.
- 1 passes to 5 without walking.
- 5 passes back to 1 for the lay-up.
- 2 rebounds and passes to 5, and 2 begins sprinting.
- The drill continues in this fashion. The ball must never be allowed to touch the floor. Doing so compels sprinting at full speed.

Rotations: 1 takes 5's place after 5 has passed to 2. 2 takes 4's place after 4 has passed to 1. 5 goes to the end of 2's line, and 4 goes to the end of 1's line.

Drill #21: Shooting, Passing, and Touch Passing

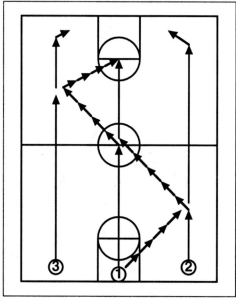

Diagram 2-8

Positions: 1, 2, 3
Number of Players: 3
Time: 1 minute

Description:
- Ball is passed 1 to 2 to 1 to 3 to 1, and so on, all the way down court.
- 2 and 3 stop about 10 to 12 feet from the basket at 45-degree angles, or at short corner.
- 1 passes to either 2 or 3, who takes the shot. If you are working on touch passing, (Drill #19), then 2 or 3 would pass back to 1 and cut. 1 would pass to the other wing and cut opposite the first cut.
- The other wing rebounds the shot and passes out to 1, who stopped at the free-throw line.
- The three players pass the ball back down the floor and repeat either the shooting procedure or the touch-passing routine.

Rotations: 1 to 2 to 3 to 1. Then continue the drill back down the floor.

Drill #22: Passing and Slide Step

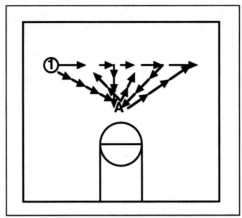

Diagram 2-9

Positions: 1, 2, 3, 4, 5
Number of Players: 2
Time: 1 minute

Description:

- 1 passes to A, then slides a step while A returns the pass to 1. 1 again passes to A and slides a step. A returns the pass. This pattern continues until 1 has gone down and back twice, and then the two players rotate.
- 1's pass can be a chest pass, a bounce pass, an overhead pass, a flip pass, or the one-handed push pass.

Rotations: 1 to A to 1.

Drill #23: Wall Passing

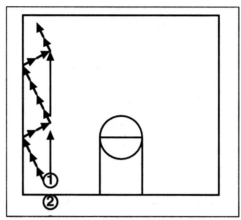

Diagram 2-10

Positions: 1, 2, 3, 4, 5
Number of Players: 1
Time: 30 seconds

Description:

- 1 passes off the wall and slides (or races) to catch it. Immediately 1 again passes off the wall and slides to receive it. This pattern continues until 1 reaches opposite sideline.
- 2 begins after 1 receives his first pass.
- 3 begins after 2 has received his first pass, and so forth.
- This pattern continues until all players reach the opposite sideline.
- Players can now return, sliding left instead of right. This step can be run several trips down and back.
- Players may use chest pass, overhead pass, flip pass, or one-handed push pass. Players may pass higher off the wall or further out on the wall (which would require a sprint to catch it).
- Players must not let the ball touch the floor.

Drill #24: Skip Passing and Shooting

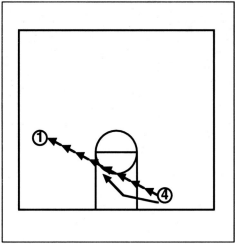

Diagram 2-11

Diagram 2-12

Positions: 1, 2, 3, 4, 5
Number of Players: 2
Time: 30 seconds

Description:
- Diagram 2-11 shows the skip pass from post in short corner. 4 skip passes to 1. 1 can be placed where the opening occurs in your next opponent's zone defense. 1 can shoot a jump shot. 4 would crash the boards.
- If 1 does not shoot, 4 flash pivots for the pass from 1 and a turn-around jump shot. Both 1 and 4 crash the boards.
- Diagram 2-12 depicts 1 replacing himself after he has passed into the cutting 4. 4 passes to 1 for a three-point attempt. These occurrences are frequent against zone defenses.

Drill #25: Baseball Pass and Dribbling Lay-Up

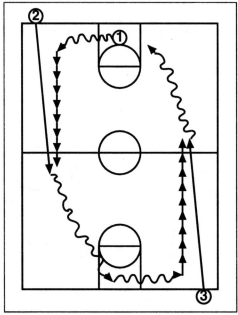

Diagram 2-13

Positions: 1, 2, 3
Number of Players: 3
Time: 2 minutes

Description:
- 1 dribbles to the corner and throws a baseball pass to the sprinting 2.
- 2 dribbles in for a lay-up. 2 gets his own rebound, and dribbles to the corner.
- When 2 gets his rebound, 3 takes off in a sprint. When 2 reaches the corner, he throws a baseball pass to 3.
- 3 dribbles in for a lay-up. 3 gets his own rebound, and dribbles to the corner.
- When 3 gets his rebound, 1 takes off in a sprint, and the drill continues in this fashion.

Variation:
- Have players make a dribbling move before getting either the jump shot or the lay-up.

Drill #26: Fake Passing

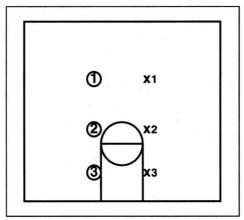

Diagram 2-14

Positions: 1, 2, 3, 4, 5
Number of Players: 2
Time: 1 minute

Description:

- 1 has a basketball. If you are using more than two players, half of them will have a basketball (2 and 3 in Diagram 2-14).
- X1, X2, and X3 stand with arms folded in front of themselves.
- 1, 2, and 3 pass the ball to X1, X2, and X3 respectively, or 1, 2, and 3 can fake a pass to X1, X2, and X3.
- You may require any pass to be used: two-handed chest pass, one-handed chest pass, overhead chest pass, bounce pass, or one-handed push pass.
- If 1's fake is good enough to get X1 to unfold his arms, 1 gets two points. If 1 passes the ball to X1, and X1 does not catch it, 1 gets one point. If 1 passes the ball and X1 catches it, X1 gets one point.
- X1, once he gets the ball, fake passes to 1. This pattern continues until either 1 or X1 reaches 12 points.

Drill #27: Spectrum Passing

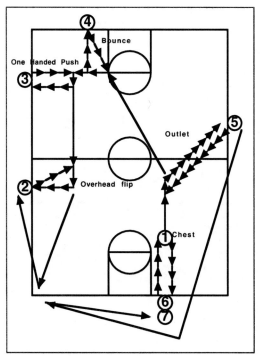

Diagram 2-15

Positions: 1, 2, 3, 4, 5
Number of Players: 7
Time: 2 minutes

Description:

- 1 goes down the court and back twice before rotating.
- 6 tosses a chest pass to 1 to begin the drill.
- 1 immediately returns a chest pass to 6.
- 1 turns to face downcourt. As 1 turns, 5 throws an outlet pass to 1. 1 immediately returns an outlet pass to 5. 1 begins a sprint down the floor. 5 sprints to baseline left corner where he deposits his basketball (after 1's second trip). 1 will retrieve this ball at the end of 1's two trips. 2, 3, and 4 keep their basketballs as they rotate.
- When 1 gets to the free-throw line, 4 tosses a bounce pass to 1. 1 throws a bounce pass back to 4. 1 turns to face downcourt.
- When 1 turns to face downcourt, 3 tosses a one-handed push pass to 1. 1 immediately returns a one-handed push pass to 3.

- 1 begins a sprint down the floor. When 1 reaches half-court, 2 lobs an overhead flip pass to 1. 1 immediately returns the overhead flip pass to 2, and 1 sprints to the baseline where he picks up a basketball and sprints to 2's position.

Variations:

- Instead of player 1 making the same pass back to the player from whom he receives the pass, player 1 shoots the ball, and the original passer offensively rebounds it.
- Instead of shooting the ball, player 1 and the original passer go one-on-one. In this case, player 1 must score three of the six times, or he must go again.

Rotations: 1 to 2 to 3 to 4 to 5 to 6 to 7 to 1.

Drill #28: Diamond Passing

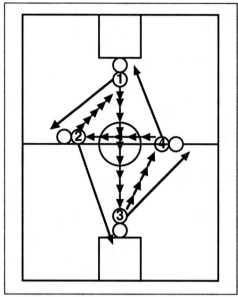

Diagram 2-16

Positions: 1, 2, 3, 4, 5
Number of Players: 8
Time: 2 minutes

Description:

- Line players up as shown in Diagram 2-16. 1 begins with a basketball. 1 throws an outlet pass to 3.
- 3 throws a bounce pass to 4.
- 4 tosses a chest pass to 2.
- 2 flips an overhead lob to the next player in 1's line.
- As soon as a player passes, he moves to the end of the line where he is rotating.

Variation:

- Move players 1 and 3 closer together (about 15 feet apart) and allow players to fake passing to any line they choose. Then they make a pass and rotate to the end of the line where they passed.

Rotation: 1 to 2 to 3 to 4 (original drill, not the variation).

Drill #29: Four-Corner Passing

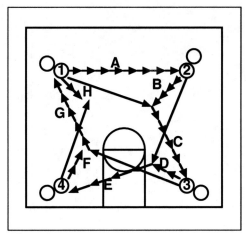

Diagram 2-17

Positions: 1, 2, 3, 4, 5
Number of Players: 8
Time: 2 minutes

Description:

- 1 passes to 2 and sprints toward 2 (pass A). 2 passes back to 1 (pass B). 1 passes to 3 while 2 sprints toward 3 (pass C). 1 goes to the end of 2's line.
- 3 passes to 2 (pass D). 2 passes to 4 while 3 sprints toward 4 (pass E). 2 goes to the end of 3's line.
- You may require any pass or mix them up.
- This procedure and rotation continues around the four corners.
- Reverse directions after one minute.

Rotations: 1 to 2 to 3 to 4 to 1.

Drill #30: Two-Player Rapid Fire

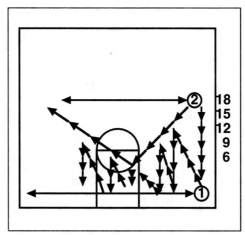

Diagram 2-18

Positions: 1, 2, 3, 4, 5
Number of Players: 2
Time: 1 minute

Description:
- 1 slides along the baseline, receiving a pass from 2 and passing back to 2.
- 2 begins 18 feet away, and after each pass, 2 moves in toward 1 until 2 gets six feet away from 1. When 2 gets within six feet, 2 again slides to 18 feet away from 1. When 2 gets 18 feet away from 1, 1 and 2 change directions, and 2 begins to move back toward 1 after each pass.
- 2 goes down and back twice before 1 and 2 rotate.
- The passes are as follows:

18 feet	Overhead
15 feet	Chest
12 feet	Bounce
9 feet	Lob
6 feet	Touch
9 feet	Lob
12 feet	Overhead flip lob outlet
15 feet	Overhead flip
18 feet	Baseball

Drill #31: Team Post Passing

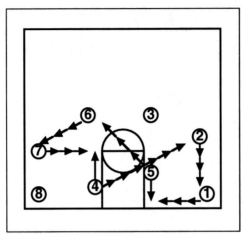

Diagram 2-19

Positions: 4, 5
Number of Players: 8
Time: 2 minutes

Description:
- Start by using two balls. Both 5 and 4 begin with a ball.
- 4 can pass only to 1, 2, or 3; 5 can pass only to 6, 7, or 8.
- Once the post player passes the ball, he adjusts slightly for the next pass. Doing so allows the post player to pass from all side-post, low-post, and short-corner positions.
- In Diagram 2-19, 5 passes to 6 while 4 passes to 2. This pass often occurs against zone defenses. Diagram 2-19 continues with a pass from 6 to 7 and 4 adjusting for a pass from 7. The diagram also depicts 2 passing to 1, and 5 adjusting for a pass from 1.
- The perimeter players should cut slightly after each pass into a post position. When the post player receives a pass, he pivots and looks opposite. Post players may pass to either of the three perimeter players.

Variation:
- Coach can allow outside players to shoot on a certain number of passes, compelling 4 and 5 to rebound offensively.

Rotations: After one minute, 4 and 5 exchange sides of the court.

Drill #32: Two-on-One Passing

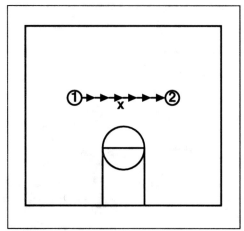

Diagram 2-20

Positions: 1, 2, 3, 4, 5
Number of Players: 3
Time: 1 minute

Description:

- Divide squad into units of three players. One player begins on defense. Defender must play equal distance from the two passers.
- Players must fake pass before they pass.
- If the defender tips the pass, the defender replaces the attacker who threw the pass. The attacker becomes the new defender.
- All passes except the lobs can be practiced.

Variation:

- Passers may dribble one or two dribbles in either direction, and then throw a pass. The receiver may stay or slide with the passer by using a cut.

Drill #33: Combo Overhead and Chest Passing

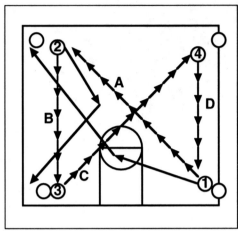

Diagram 2-21

Positions: 1, 2, 3, 4, 5
Number of Players: 8
Time: 2 minutes

Description:
- Line players up as shown in Diagram 2-21.
- 1 throws overhead outlet pass to 2. 2 tosses a chest pass to 3. 3 responds with an overhead outlet pass to 4, and 4 pitches a chest pass to first player in the line 1 just left.
- After each player makes his pass, he uses a V-cut to the end of the line where they passed. This cut must be done quickly so the next passer will not hit the cutter with a pass.

Rotations: 1 to end of line 2, 2 to end of line 3, 3 to end of line 4, and 4 to the end of line 1

Drill #34: Pepper Passing

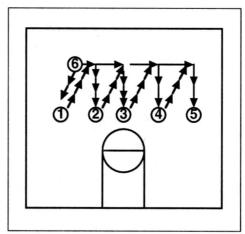

Diagram 2-22

Positions: 1, 2, 3, 4, 5
Number of Players: 6
Time: 3 minutes

Description:
- Line players up as depicted in Diagram 2-22.
- 6 passes to 1 who passes back to 6 who passes to 2 who passes back to 6 who passes to 3. This pattern continues until 6 slides down the line and back. 6 is about 12 feet from the line.
- 6 goes down and back before he takes 5's place and the others slide down one spot. At this point, 1 becomes the new 6.

Variations:
- You can require greater concentration by using two balls. Let 6 begin with a ball and let 1 begin with a ball. 6 passes to 2 while 1 is passing to 6. Upon receiving the pass from 1, 6 passes that ball to 3. Meanwhile, 2 is passing back to 6. This pattern continues down and back before the previous rotation occurs. You can stipulate that each player goes down and back twice before a rotation occurs.
- Place a defender between the sliding 6 and the line with five passers. Now the drill slows down, but fake passing must occur.

Rotations: 1 to 2 to 3 to 4 to 5 to 6 to 1

3

Dribbling

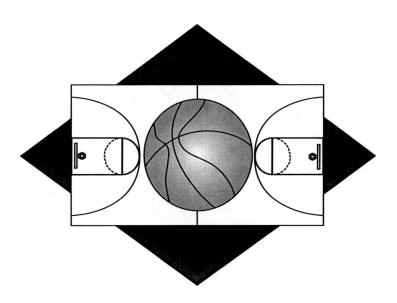

Drill #35: Advanced Dribble Slap

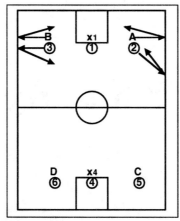

Diagram 3-1

Positions: 1, 2, 3, 4, 5
Number of Players: 12
Time: 3 minutes

Description:
- Both 1 and X1 start with two basketballs (as does 4 and X4 on the other side of the court).
- 1 and X1 try to slap away one of the basketballs in any direction.
- A is paired with 2, B with 3, C with 5, and D with 6. These eight players are making V-cuts to the sidelines and back.
- Once a ball is slapped outside the free-throw circle by either 1 or X1 (4 and X4 on the other end), the pair nearest the slapped ball battle to recover it. For example, if the ball is slapped toward A and 2, the player who recovers it goes on offense while the other player defends in a one-on-one game.
- The second ball must be fought for by B and 3. When the third ball is slapped away, 1 and X1 go one-on-one (the player with the ball is on offense). This last one-on-one maneuver is a full-court one-on-one battle.

Variation:
- Give all players a basketball. The players outside the circle dribble to and from the sidelines until they spot a deflection inside the circle (by either 1 or X1), then they leave their dribble and go battle for the recovery.

Rotations: Squads of two rotate:
- 1 and X1 to 2 and A to 3 and B to 1 and X1
- 4 and X4 to 5 and C to 6 and D to 4 and X4

Drill #36: Full-Court Recovery

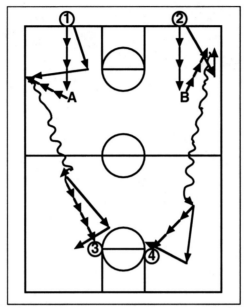

Diagram 3-2

Positions: 1, 2, 3, 4, 5
Number of Players: 6
Time: 2 minutes

Description:
- 1 passes to A. A rolls the ball on the floor somewhere away from 1. 1 uses a V-cut to go get the ball (backdoor cut if ball is rolled behind 1).
- 1 speed dribbles down the floor (or uses a dribble move if the coach prefers).
- 1 passes to 3. 1 uses another V-cut to break off 3's screen for a pass and a jump shot.
- Instead of passing to 3, 3 can set a screen for 1 to drive around. 3 can now activate the screen and roll.
- Instead of a jump shot, 1 can use an offensive move (spin dribble, for example) to drive for a lay-up.
- The same procedures are available for 2 and 4 on the other side of the court.
- Players go down the floor and back before they rotate.

Rotations:
- 1 to A to 3 to 1
- 2 to B to 4 to 2

Drill #37: Skip Pass and Penetration

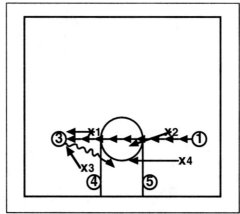

Diagram 3-3

Positions: 1, 2, 3, 4, 5
Number of Players: 8
Time: 2 minutes

Description:
- Line up four offensive and four defensive players as shown in Diagram 3-3.
- 1 and 3 skip pass while the defenders slide in direction of the pass.
- Whenever 1 or 3 can dribble penetrate by their two defenders, they do so.
- In Diagram 3-3, 3 dribble penetrates by X3 and X4. At this point, X1 and X2 must cover 3, 4, and 5. 3 must make correct decisions: shoot, pass to 4, pass to 5, or pass back out to 1. If the pass is to 4 or 5, those players make a move, shoot, or skip pass back to the perimeter player on the weakside. If pass is to 1, 1 can follow his reception with a shot, or another dribble penetration, or a skip pass back to 3 who has relocated.

Variation:
- You can allow the lower defender (X3 in Diagram 3-3) to help defend the inside once 3 drives by X1 and X3. This option not only simulates what will actually happen in a ballgame, but it impels 3 to make an even better choice.

Rotations: After one minute of drilling, 1 and 3 become X1 and X2, and 4 and 5 become X3 and X4. X1 becomes 3, X2 takes 1's spot, X3 replaces 4, and X4 is the new 5.

Drill #38: Dribble, Pivot, and Pass Team

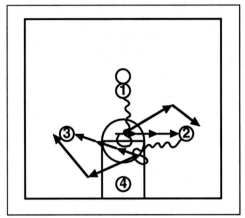

Diagram 3-4

Positions: 1, 2, 3
Number of Players: 5
Time: 1 minute

Description:
- Line players up as shown in Diagram 3-4.
- In Diagram 3-4, 1 dribbles to middle, pivots, and passes to 2. 1 could have pivoted and passed to either 3 or 4. 1 goes to the end of the line where he passed (2 in Diagram 3-4). This movement to the end of the receiver's line should be a V-cut.
- Once 2 receives the pass, 2 dribbles to middle, pivots, and passes to 3. 2 could have passed to 1 or 4, as well. 2 V-cuts to the end of 3's line (in Diagram 3-4).
- The drill continues in this sequence.

Variation:
- Put X1 in the middle of the court. X1 defends the dribble, pivot, and pass. You can require X1 to deflect the pass before he becomes an offensive player, or you can allow X1 to rotate to offense while the dribbler/passer becomes the new defender.

Drill #39: Recovery Lay-Up

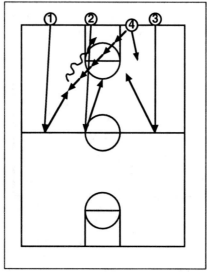

Diagram 3-5

Positions: 1, 2, 3
Number of Players: 4
Time: 1 minute

Description:
- 1, 2, and 3 sprint to the half-court line then sprint back toward the basket. All players use the V-cut to come back to the basket.
- 4 passes the ball to one of the players when he reaches the area near the top of the key. Player receiving the pass dribble drives hard to the basket for a lay-up (1 in Diagram 3-5).
- The other two players (2 and 3 in Diagram 3-5) try to stop the lay-up.
- If the shot is missed, all three players battle for the offensive rebound. Pump fakes may be used to score.
- When a score occurs, the players rotate and the three would-be attackers sprint to half-court, using a V-cut to come back to the basket.

Variation:
- 4 steps onto the court and plays offense with the pass receiver in a two-on-two game. 1 (in Diagram 3-5) has several options at this point: he can pass to 4, who can make a move and shoot or pass back to 1, he can continue in for the lay-up with 4 hitting the offensive boards, or he can take a jump shot. 2 and 3 must box out.

Rotations: 1 to 2 to 3 to 4 to 1

Drill #40: Three Drill Defensively

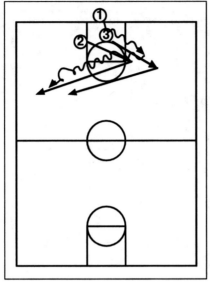

Diagram 3-6

Positions: 1, 2, 3
Number of Players: 3
Time: 2 minutes

Description:
- 1 tries to dribble the length of the court against 2 and 3 (Diagram 3-6). 1 must learn to keep his dribble alive.
- 2 and 3 try to trap 1 and make him pick up his dribble.
- If either 2 or 3 steal the dribble, they fast break two-on-one against 1.
- 1 must use speed dribble, control dribble, hesitation dribble, retreat dribble, change of pace, or change of direction to try to split 2 and 3 or to try to drive outside either 2 or 3. 1 tries to score when he reaches the far end of the court.
- 1 goes against 2 and 3 down and back before the players rotate.

Variations:
- Put another player on the floor (4) to be an outlet pass receiver for 1, in the event that 1 has to pick up his dribble. 4 can only receive the pass from 1 and pass back to 1. 1 must use cuts to free himself for the return pass. Both 2 and 3 can double-team 1 to keep him from getting the ball back.
- Use 4 as a screen/outlet for 1. This variation brings screening into the drill.

Rotations: 1 to 2 to 3 to 1

Drill #41: Zig Zag With a Passer—Full Court

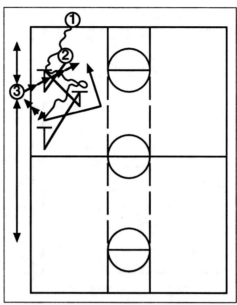

Diagram 3-7

Positions: 1, 2, 3, 4, 5
Number of Players: 3
Time: 2 minutes

Description:

- Divide the court into three vertical lanes. Put your better dribblers, like point guards, in the middle lane. Each lane will use the same procedure, but for explanation purposes this section will use only the first lane (Diagram 3-7). Match the players up so players with equal dribbling skills are in the same lane.
- The boundaries are the sidelines and the imaginary lines from free-throw-lane lines to free-throw-lane lines. Dribblers must stay inside their boundary lines.
- Diagram 3-7 depicts 1 trying to dribble by 2. 2 must turn 1's direction every 15 feet or so. A turn is a change of direction move (crossover, spin, half spin, in and out, etc.).
- Coach can make it more difficult by requiring only a certain move or sets of moves by the dribbler.
- Once 1 reaches half-court, 1 passes to 3. Now 2 tries to prevent 1 from getting the pass back from 3. This pass back must occur near the original free-throw line. Now 1 has the added pressure of trying to get the ball and dribbling across the half-court line within 10 seconds from his beginning.

- Once 1 has received the pass back from 3, 1 zig zags up to the far free-throw line. Now 1 passes again to 3. 1 again attempts to get the pass back from 3, but must receive it near the half-court line.
- Once 1 has again received the pass from 3, 1 and 2 zig zag to the end line.
- Players stay in this same pattern until 1 has gone down and back twice, and then they rotate.

Variation:
- 3 receives pass from 1, but instead of 1 trying to get open to get a pass back from 3, 3 sets a screen on 2 and tries to hand the ball off to 1. 3 must be in the lane for this screening drill.

Rotations: 1 to 2 to 3 to 1

Drill #42: Dribble Slap

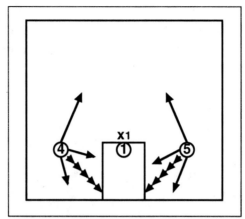

Diagram 3-8

Positions: 1, 2, 3, 4, 5
Number of Players: 4
Time: 1 minute

Description:
- 1 and X1 start with two basketballs. They must keep the dribble alive with both basketballs. 4 and 5 each have a basketball and are shooting at the goal nearest 1 and X1. If 4 or 5 misses his shot, he must go get the offensive rebound, pump fake, and power the ball back up to the basket. Both 4 and 5 should be practicing dribbling moves prior to their shots (spin, half-spin, crossover, in and out, etc.).
- 1 and X1 cannot move out of the circle at the free-throw line.
- Each player tries to slap the other player's dribble out of the circle.
- When a ball is slapped outside the circle, 4 or 5 must retrieve it. The player nearest the ball retrieves it and dribbles it along with the ball he has been shooting into the circle, replacing the player with only one ball. The player with only one ball begins shooting at the basket near the dribblers. The two players inside the circle continue to dribble two balls and try to slap the opponent's ball away.
- At the end of one minute, the player with two balls in the circle is the winner. The other players must make three trips up and down the floor using dribbling moves, speed dribbles, control dribbles, change of pace, hesitation moves, retreat dribble, and so forth.

Drill #43: Two-Ball Pivoting and Dribbling

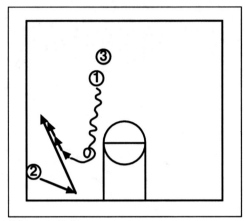

Diagram 3-9

Positions: 1, 2, 3
Number of Players: 3
Time: 1 minute

Description:
- Line players up as shown in Diagram 3-9.
- 1 dribbles toward 2.
- On this dribble toward 2, 1 can execute a dribbling move, change of pace, hesitation, or retreat dribble.
- 1 jump stops, pivots, and passes to the cutting 2, or 2 can dip and come behind 1's screen.
- After passing to 2, 1 can screen and roll if the coach so desires.
- 1 goes to the end of 2's line.
- 2 begins dribbling toward 3 where the previous procedures are repeated.

Rotations: 1 to 2 to 3 to 1.

Drill #44: Dribble, Pass, and Cut

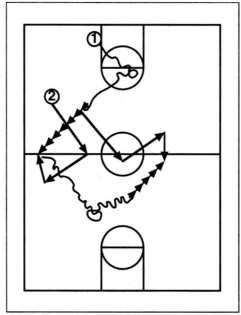

Diagram 3-10

Positions: 1, 2, 3
Number of Players: 2
Time: 1 minute

Description:
- 1 and 2 face each other about 10 feet apart (Diagram 3-10).
- 1 begins dribbling, using either a dribbling move, a speed dribble, or a control dribble.
- 2 reacts by backpedaling at the same rate of speed as 1 dribbles.
- After about 15 feet, and after having made a dribbling move, 1 passes to 2 on the move. 2 can make a V-cut, a backdoor cut, or a flash-pivot cut.
- 2 now begins dribbling toward 1. 1 backpedals at the same rate of speed as 2 dribbles, and the drill continues.

Drill #45: Dribble Tag

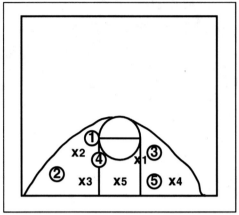

Diagram 3-11

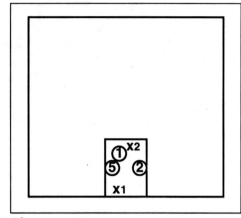

Diagram 3-12

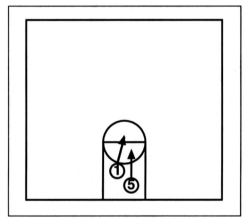

Diagram 3-13

Positions: 1, 2, 3, 4, 5
Number of Players: 10
Time: 2 minutes

Description:

- Put all 10 players inside the three-point arc. Each player begins dribbling a basketball. Any player can slap away a ball from any other player. In fact, two players can agree to double-team a dribbler, thereby eliminating one player (Diagram 3-11).
- When the dribblers get down to five in number, the dribblers move to the foul lane. Again the players cannot get outside the limited area without disqualifying themselves (Diagram 3-12).

- When the dribblers get down to two in number, they move to the free-throw circle (Diagram 3-13).
- A ball must be slapped outside the area in order to disqualify a dribbler.
- Once a dribbler is disqualified, he moves to another basket and begins to use a move, then shoot, and then rebound.
- When two dribblers are disqualified, they form a partnership and begin a line about 15 feet apart, running and passing from sideline to sideline on the other half of the court, or the two disqualified players form a line about 15 feet apart and begin to make cuts before receiving a pass from their partner.

Variations:
- Instead of all 10 players being for themselves, divide the squad into two teams. In this way, teams play and plan together to get rid of the other squad (in Diagram 3-11, the X's against the O's).
- Instead of letting each player begin with one ball, let each player begin by using two balls. In this way, the player can become disqualified by losing one ball or by losing two balls (coach's call).
- Begin by letting all players but one start with two balls. The one player with one ball is "it". This one player is the only player who can force the elimination of another player by slapping away one ball of any of the other players. When any player gets down to one ball, he helps "it" slap away other player's balls.

Drill #46: Dribble Lay-Up

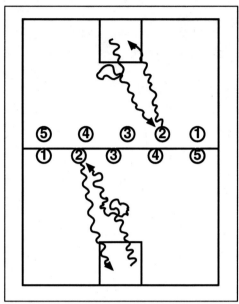

Diagram 3-14

Positions: 1, 2, 3, 4, 5
Number of Players: 10
Time: 2 minutes

Description:
- Line players up as shown in Diagram 3-14. Every player begins with a basketball.
- Number the players by their positions: point guard (1), shooting guard (2), small forward (3), power forward (4), and post (5).
- In Diagram 3-14, 2 is the number called by the coach. 2 drives for a lay-up. 2 rebounds his own shot. 2 executes a move back to his original spot.
- While 2 is driving for his lay-up, another number is called. This drill should be a rapid-movement drill, so keep calling the numbers.

Variations:
- Instead of using a speed dribble to drive for the lay-up, 2 can use a dribbling move, and then shoot a lay-up or a jump shot.
- Instead of driving for a lay-up, 2 passes to the coach, makes a cut without the ball for a pass back from the coach, and then drives for the lay-up or uses a dribbling move for the lay-up or jump shot.

4

Moves

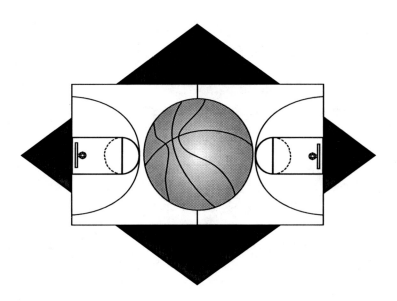

Drill #47: Creating Perimeter Space

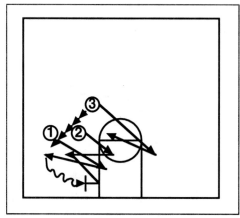

Diagram 4-1

Positions: 1, 2, 3
Number of Players: 3
Time: 5 minutes

Description:
- Line players up as shown in Diagram 4-1.
- 1 V-cuts to get open while 2 defends. 3 passes to 1 when he gets open. 1 squares up and attacks 2.
- 1 does not take a bad shot. If 1 cannot create space for the shot, 1 passes to 3, and 1 begins his cutting maneuvers to get open again.
- 1 is allowed only three dribbles to free himself for a shot.

Variations:
- 1 goes against 2 for three consecutive times. If 1 fails to create space in two of the three times, 1 goes to defense and stays on defense for the remainder of the drill, or until the next offensive player fails to create space two of three times.
- 1 goes against 2 for three consecutive times. 1 must score on two of those possessions or 1 goes on defense and stays until the next offensive player fails to score on two of three times. The attacker may hit the offensive boards and score should he miss the shot.

Rotations: 1 to 2 to 3 to 1

Drill #48: Three Big Men Post Moves

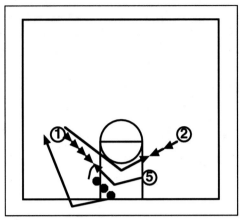

Diagram 4-2

Positions: 4, 5
Number of Players: 3
Time: 5 minutes

Description:
- In this three-men pivot shooting and moves drill, both 1 and 2 begin with a basketball (Diagram 4-2).
- 5 flash pivots toward 1. 1 overhead flip (or bounce) passes to 5. 5 pivots and shoots. 5 can use a move (such as drop step baseline, face-up, spin, half-spin, etc.), and then shoot. 5 rebounds his own shot and hurries out to replace 1. You can demand that the post rebound his miss shots, pump fake, and power the lay-up.
- Meanwhile 1 has gone to big block on right side and flash pivots toward 2. 2 hits 1 with an overhead (or bounce) pass. 1 pivots (or uses a move) and shoots. 1 rebounds his own shot and replaces 2.
- Meanwhile 2 has gone to big block on the left side and flash pivots toward 5 (remember: 5 has replaced 1). The drill continues for five minutes of moves and shooting.
- Upon receiving pass from the wing, the post player can use the drop steps, the half spins, the spin, the face-ups, the power moves, and so forth. The coach can determine which moves to use, or let the post man determine for himself.

Variation:
- You can add a defender. In this case, the defender would replace the passer, and the post attacker would become the next defender.

Drill #49: Two-Line Moves and Shooting

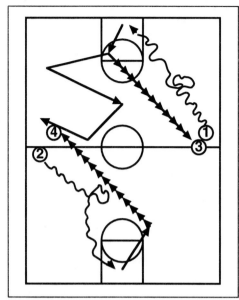

Diagram 4-3

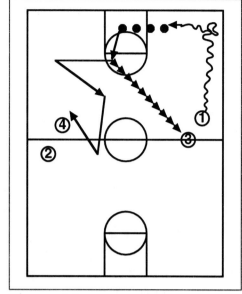

Diagram 4-4

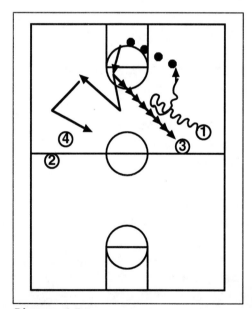

Diagram 4-5

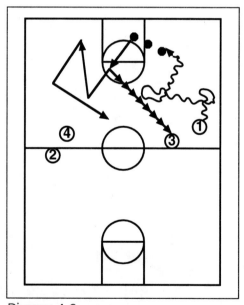

Diagram 4-6

Positions: 1, 2, 3
Number of Players: 4
Time: 4 minutes

Description:

- Begin sequence of drills with two lines as shown in Diagram 4-3.

- 1 and 2 use a dribbling move and shoot, rebound, and pass to the next player in line. Change the distance from the basket daily, which allows for baseball pass on one day and a chest or bounce pass on the next. Player in one line rotates to the back of the other line after he passes.

- In Diagram 4-3, both 1 and 2 use a dribbling move and drive all the way for a lay-up—one side using the sideline route, and the other side using the middle route.

- Diagram 4-4 exhibits dribbler stopping for the jump shot. Only 1's movement is shown for simplicity of explanation.

- Diagram 4-5 illustrates a reverse, crossover, half spin, or in-and-out dribbling move followed by jump shot. These moves should occur from different spots on different days.

- Diagram 4-6 demonstrates two different dribbling moves before the shot. These moves should occur in rapid succession using no more than four dribbles.

- By beginning the lines at the three-point arc, players can perform the different phases of the rocker step before the dribbling move or before shooting off the rocker step.

- When moving from one line to the other, player should use different cuts: flash-pivot cut, sideline V-cut, and so forth.

Drill #50: One-Line Offensive Moves

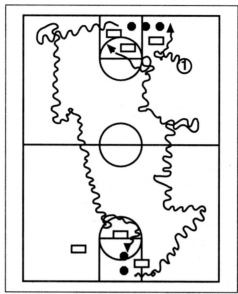

Diagram 4-7

Positions: 1, 2, 3
Number of Players: 1
Time: 3 minutes

Description:
- Begin with a single player and two or three chairs (or cones, etc.) placed at different spots near the scoring area.
- 1 dribbles hard toward the first chair. 1 uses crossover, spin, half spin, or in and out. If 1 uses spin first time, then 1 should use a different move the second time.
- 1 rebounds his shot (if missed, 1 can use pump fakes and power lay-ups). 1 dribbles hard to another area on the court (using a speed dribble once, a controlled dribble another time, a change of pace, a hesitation dribble, or a retreat dribble).
- At this point, the player is in position to begin another dribbling move toward the basket. The player keeps this move going for three minutes. The player should drive right for a while, and then drive left.

Variation:
- Instead of using chairs, a defender can be placed on the court at each of the chair locations. The attacker must use the dribbling move dictated by the defender's stance and positioning.

Drill #51: Full-Court Feed the Post

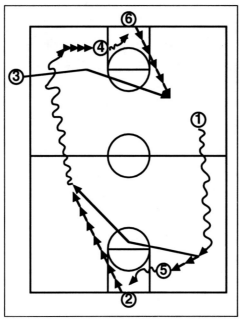

Diagram 4-8

Positions: 1, 2, 3, 4, 5
Number of Players: 6
Time: 3 minutes

Description:

- Line players up as shown in Diagram 4-8.
- 1 begins the drill by driving hard to an area below the free-throw line extended where 1 can get a perfect passing angle inside to 5. 1 passes inside to 5, and 1 dips to an open perimeter area for a possible pass back from 5. If 5 passes back to 1, 1 can shoot or find another passing angle back into the posting 5.
- In Diagram 4-8, 5 drop steps and shoots a lay-up. This move is 1's key to run a diagonal cut across the court. 2 rebounds 5's shot and outlet passes to the cutting 1. 1 drives down the left sideline to an area below the free-throw line extended. 1 passes inside to the posting 4. 1 V-cuts to an open perimeter area for a possible pass back from 4.
- 4 or 1 makes a move and shoots. 6 rebounds and 3 runs a diagonal cut for an outlet pass from 6. 3 dribbles down the right sideline, and the drill continues in this fashion.

Variations:

- You can add a defender on the post player. In this case 6 defends 4 and 2 defends 5. Then they rotate from offense to defense to offense, which makes the post part of the drill competitive.
- You can add screening to the drill by allowing the perimeter player who passes to the post to cut off the post for a return pass and a screen-and-roll maneuver. Or the post player can pass back to the perimeter player and then the post goes to screen for the perimeter player.
- You can have 3 step onto the court while 1 is bringing the ball down the court. 1 can pass to 3 immediately, or 1 and 3 can work on a triangle set up with the post for passing before the entry pass into the post. 1 and 3 can work screening maneuvers as well. If you want the same action on the other side of the court, you will need to add a seventh player (positioned where 3 is, except on the far end of the court and on the opposite side).

Rotations:

- 1 to 3 to 1
- 4 to 6 to 4
- 2 to 5 to 2

Drill #52: Three-Perimeter Moves and Shooting

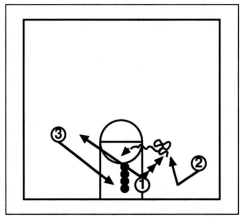

Diagram 4-9

Positions: 1, 2, 3
Number of Players: 3
Time: 2 minutes

Description:
- 1 begins with a basketball (Diagram 4-9).
- 1 passes to 2, who has V-cut to an open spot.
- 2 makes a move and shoots. 3 crashes the offensive boards. 1 has moved outside to find an open spot.
- 3 rebounds and passes to 1, who has V-cut to an open spot.
- 1 makes an offensive move and shoots. 2 crashes the offensive boards. 3 has moved outside to find an open spot. The drill continues in this routine.

Variations:
- Instead of making the pass out to the next shooter, the pass can be made to the player who shot the ball. This player then passes to the next shooter, who cuts before he receives the pass. Then the passer crashes the offensive boards, and the drill continues.
- Instead of the original shooter passing to the next shooter, the next shooter goes and screens for the rebounder. At this point, the rebounder is the next shooter. The drill continues in this sequence.

Drill #53: The Killer Attack

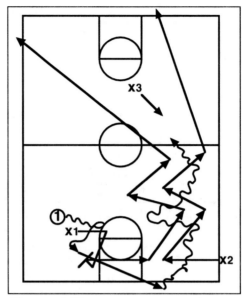

Diagram 4-10

Positions: 1, 2, 3
Number of Players: 4
Time: 3 minutes

Description:

- 1 goes one on one against X1 (Diagram 4-10).
- If 1 misses the shot, he crashes the offensive boards. X1 must box out.
- 1 takes the ball out of bounds. 1 must attack X1 and X2 in a two-on-one drill to half-court.
- When 1 crosses half-court, X1 and X2 drop off, and 1 begins a one-on-one dribble attack against X3.
- If 1 misses the shot, he crashes the boards. X3 must box out.
- X1 and X2 have raced to the end line where 1 is playing X3 one-on-one. 1 takes the ball out of bounds, and 1 must defeat X1 and X2 to half-court on a dribble.
- When 1 crosses half-court, 1 attacks X3, who has raced down the floor while 1 is dribbling against X1 and X2. The players rotate, and the drill continues.

Variation:

- 1 must accomplish four of his five sequences, or 1 must go again.

Rotations: 1 to X3 to X2 to X1 to 1

Drill #54: Continuous Moves and Shooting

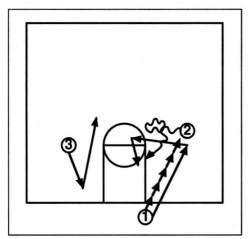

Diagram 4-11

Positions: 1, 2, 3
Number of Players: 3
Time: 5 minutes

Description:
- 1 passes to 2. 1 closes out to 2, and they go one-on-one.
- 2 makes an offensive move, creates space, and shoots within three dribbles.
- 1 stays at 2's spot, and simulates making a cut to get open.
- 2 rebounds shot and passes to 3.
- 2 closes out on 3, and they go one-on-one.
- Score is kept to see who scores the most within five minutes.

Variation:
- 1 and 2 battle for the offensive rebound should 2 miss the shot. Whoever gets the offensive basket goes to 2's original spot. The other player passes the ball out to 3 and closes out on 3. In this way, the offensive player stays on offense until he is stopped.

Drill #55: Perimeter Moves and Screening

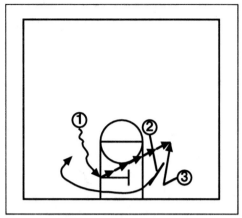

Diagram 4-12

Positions: 1, 2, 3
Number of Players: 3
Time: 5 minutes

Description:

- 1 makes a rocker-step move, followed by a dribbling move. He then passes to 3.
- 2 screens for 3 while 1 is making his dribbling move.
- After 1 passes to 3, 3 makes a rocker-step move, followed by a dribbling move.
- After 1 passes to 3, 1 finds 2 and goes screens for 2.
- 3 passes to 2, and 3 then looks to find 1. 3 screens for 1 as 2 begins his dribbling move.
- 2 first does a rocker-step move, and then a dribbling move. The drill continues in this fashion.

Variations:

- Instead of making a rocker-step move, the receiver of the pass can shoot as he comes off of the screen.
- Instead of making a rocker-step move, the receiver can make a zone fake (like fake a shot, dribble right or left, or penetrate and pass back outside).

Drill #56: Continuous Moves

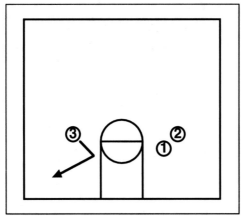

Diagram 4-13

Positions: 1, 2, 3
Number of Players: 3
Time: 5 minutes

Description:
- 2 begins with a basketball, and 1 defends 2. This drill can start as token defense with 2 working on his rocker step, and then it should become a live drill.
- 2 makes a move (first without allowing a dribble, then allow two dribbles, then advance to three dribbles). 2 shoots.
- 1 and 2 battle on the boards.
- Meanwhile 3 has made a V-cut to get a pass from 1.
- 2 goes out and defends 3, and the drill continues.

Variation:
- When 1 stops 2, 1 takes the ball out of bounds. 2 immediately tries to prevent the inbounds pass to 3. 3 must make a move to get open. Once 3 receives the pass, 3 makes a move while 2 defends, and the drill continues.

Drill #57: Individual Perimeter Moves

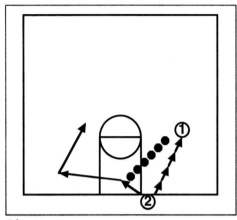

Diagram 4-14

Diagram 4-15

Positions: 1, 2, 3
Number of Players: 2
Time: 5 minutes

Description:
- 2 passes to 1. 1 performs the following rocker step series, shooting after each phase: jab step, jump shot; jab step, pull back, jump shot; jab step, pull back, direct drive; jab step, pull back, crossover drive. 2 rebounds each phase. 1 performs the entire series with his left foot as pivot foot, and then with his right foot as pivot foot. On the last stage, 2 uses a V-cut to find an open spot on the perimeter. 1 rebounds his own shot (last shot) and passes out to 2, who performs each phase of the rocker step while 1 rebounds (Diagram 4-14).
- On his last shot, 2 follows for the rebound while 1 V-cuts for a pass from 2. The drill continues this way for five minutes.

Variations:
- 2 passes to 1 and steps in to rebound while 1 executes the dribbling moves: crossover dribble, spin dribble, half-spin dribble, in-and-out maneuver. 2 rebounds each shot while 1 relocates. On 1's last move, 1 rebounds his own shot, and 2 V-cuts to an open spot on the perimeter. 1 passes to 2, and 2 executes the dribble moves. The drill continues in this fashion for five minutes (Diagram 4-15).
- You could have 1 execute the rocker step, exchange places with 2 while 2 uses the rocker step; then the players exchange places and each executes the dribbling moves. In this way, the five minutes would be equally divided between rocker step and the dribbling moves.
- 2, in Diagram 4-15, can become a screener either for 1 to use off the dribble, or 2 can execute the screen and roll with 1.

Drill #58: Individual Post Moves

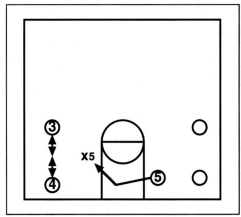

Diagram 4-16

Positions: 4, 5
Number of Players: 4
Time: 5 minutes

Description:
- 5 breaks across the lane trying to get post positioning on X5. 3 and 4 pass the ball until they can pass the ball inside to 5. No lob passes are permitted.
- Once 5 receives the pass, 5 goes one-on-one against X5.
- Before making the drill live, you can allow the post defender to play only token defense. Doing so would allow 5 to work on all his post moves: drop step inside, drop step outside, spin, half spin, power dribble, and face-ups.

Variation:
- Put two other perimeter passers on the other side of the court. 5 moves from one side of the court to the other. 5 receives a pass, executes a move, and shoots while X5 rebounds. 5 can work on only one move, like spin dribble, or he can run the full repertoire of moves. Then rotate from X5 to 5 to X5 to 5. These two players then exchange places with 3 and 4. They execute the same moves. Then 3 and 4 exchange places with the remaining two perimeter passers.

Rotations: 3 to 4 to 5 to X5 to 3.

5

Screening

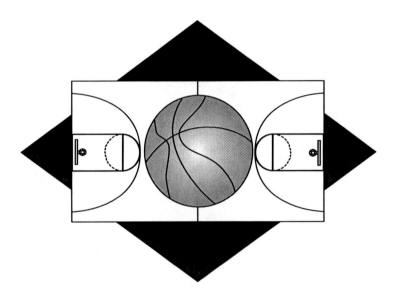

Drill #59: Full-Court Screening

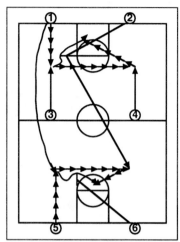

Diagram 5-1

Positions: 1, 2, 3, 4, 5
Number of Players: 6
Time: 3 minutes

Description:

- Line players up as shown in Diagram 5-1. Both 1 and 5 begin with a basketball.
- 3 and 4 begin with a controlled sprint toward 1 and 2. 1 passes to 3, who passes to 4.
- Meanwhile, 2 has set a screen for 3.
- 3 cuts off of 2's screen, and 4 passes the ball to 3 for a jump shot or a lay-up. Both 3 and 4 crash the offensive boards. Then 3 and 4 take the places of 1 and 2 at the baseline.
- As soon as 1 passes the ball to 3 and 2 sets the screen for 3, 1 and 2 begin an all-out sprint to the opposite end of the court.
- 5 passes the ball to 1, who passes the ball to 2.
- Meanwhile, 6 has set the screen for 1.
- 1 cuts off of 6's screen, and 2 passes the ball to 1 for a jump shot or a lay-up. Both 1 and 2 go hard to the offensive boards. 1 and 2 replace 5 and 6. 1 and 2 should exchange sides of the court on each trip so they can be the passer, the screener, and the shooter.
- 5 and 6 sprint hard to the opposite end of the court. And the drill continues.

Variation:

- When a player receives a pass for the jump shot, the player can make an offensive move before shooting.

Drill #60: Four-Ball Screening and Shooting

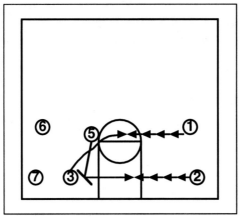

Diagram 5-2

Positions: 1, 2, 3, 4, 5
Number of Players: 6
Time: 5 minutes

Description:
- 1, 2, 6, and 7 all start with a basketball (Diagram 5-2).
- 5 screens down for 3, as shown in the diagram (other types of screens can be used instead of the screen down). 3 dips and breaks high for a pass and a jump shot. You should alter the spots on the court where your players execute the screen each day. You should change the screen you have them work on each day.
- 1 passes to 3, who shoots (or can make a move and then shoot). 3 stays high while 1 rebounds the shot.
- 2 passes to 5 as 5 rolls back to the basket. 5 shoots (or makes a move and then shoots). 5 shoots and 2 rebounds the shot.
- 1 and 2 dribble back to their positions while 3 screens down for 5.
- 6 and 7 pass the ball to 5 and 3. 5 and 3 make moves and shoot. 6 and 7 rebound the shots.
- The drill continues until 3 and 5 have taken 10 shots from each position. Then 1 and 2 take the spots of 6 and 7. 3 and 5 replace 1 and 2. And 6 and 7 become the new screeners/shooters.

Variations:

- Have 3 and 5 set dribbling screens for 1 and 2. 1 and 2 break off these screens for the jump shot or lay-up. 1 and 2 still rebound their own shots and the drill continues with 3 and 5 setting dribbling screens until all (1, 2, 6, and 7) have taken 10 shots from each position. The same rotation would occur.

- Put two defenders on the screeners. Coach can tell the defenders whether he wants them to switch or stay with their assignments. When using this option, you would want the offense to become the defense and the defense to become the offense before rotating. Then when rotating, 1 and 2 would start on offense, and 6 and 7 on defense. 3 and 5 and their defenders would become the new perimeter passers.

- Have the two passers crash the offensive boards. If you teach steps to go get the rebound, they could work on these. Once they rebound missed shots, they could be required to tip the ball, or rebound and then pump fake and shoot a power lay-up.

Drill #61: Team Continuous Screening

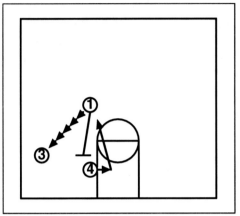

Diagram 5-3

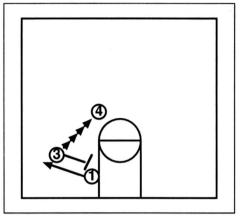

Diagram 5-4

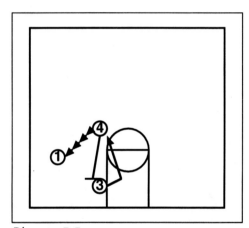

Diagram 5-5

Positions: 1, 2, 3, 4, 5
Number of Players: 3
Time: 1 minute

Description:
- Can set the screening maneuvers up anywhere. These diagrams use a point (1), a wing (3), and a post man (4).
- Diagram 5-3 shows 1 passing to 3, and 1 setting a down screen for the post man (4).
- Diagram 5-4 depicts 3 passing to 4, and 2 setting a horizontal screen for 1.
- Diagram 5-5 illustrates 4 passing to 1, and then setting a down screen for 2. This pattern continues for one minute. Make sure all players set up their screens correctly, cut off the screens correctly, and set the screens correctly.

Variation:
- Instead of screening the three players, you may operate using only cutting maneuvers.

Drill #62: Secondary Break and Screening

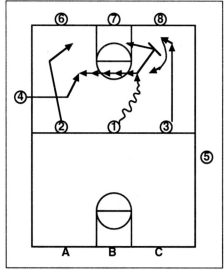

Diagram 5-6

Positions: 1, 2, 3, 4, 5
Number of Players: 11
Time: 3 minutes

Description:
- 1, 2, and 3 run a three-lane fast break. 4 fills in at half-court.
- 4 becomes the reversal receiver from 1 (which is the most popular way to reverse the ball in secondary phase of the fast break).
- 1, 2, and 3 run the options of the team fast break. In Diagram 5-6, 1 goes to set screen for 3, and then rolls to the basket.
- After the shot, made or missed, 7 outlet passes to 5. 6, 7, and 8 run the three-lane fast break. 5 fills in at mid-court to become the reversal receiver. 6, 7, and 8 run the team secondary break.
- B rebounds the missed shot, and B outlet passes to 4. 4 has sprinted back to his spot to be ready. A, B, and C fast break with 4 filling in at half-court to become the reversal receiver.
- The drill continues in this fashion for three minutes.

Drill #63: Screen-and-Roll Warm-Up

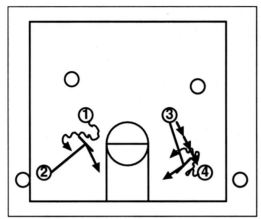

Diagram 5-7

Positions: 1, 2, 3
Number of Players: 4
Time: 1 minute

Description:
- Although Diagram 5-7 shows both sides of the half-court, you can elect to only use one side (four players instead of eight). This drill is excellent for use when you divide your squad into post and perimeter players.
- On one side of the court, two players execute the screen and roll off of the dribble. On the other side of the court, two players perform the screen and roll off of the pass. If you use only one side of the half-court, then the options can be run consecutively.
- 1 dribbles by 2's screen. 2 rolls. One of the two players shoots while both crash the offensive boards. 1 can shoot, or 1 can pass to 2, who shoots.
- 3 passes to 4 and goes to set the screen for 4. 4 drives around 3's screen as 3 rolls. One of the players shoots and both battle for the offensive rebound. 4 can shoot, or 4 can pass to 3, who shoots.
- 1 goes to the end of line 2, and 2 goes to the end of line 1. 3 goes to end of line 4, and 4 goes to end of line 3.
- Change the side of the court the following day so each screen and roll can be executed from both sides of the court.

Variation:
- Run any screening maneuver between two players.

Drill #64: Post Screening and Cutting

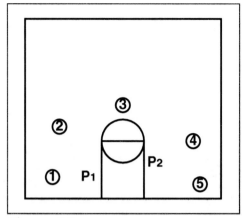

Diagram 5-8

Positions: 4, 5
Number of Players: 7
Time: 1 minute

Description:
- Line up five perimeter players and two post players (Diagram 5-8).
- The two post players (P1 and P2) must know the cuts and screens of your half-court offense.
- Two balls are used. In Diagram 5-8, 1 and 4 begin with a basketball. One ball must always be on each side of the court.
- Coach can yell out the maneuver the post players are to use: crosscourt screen, screen for wing, flash-pivot cut, and so on.
- Post executes the cut or screen, receives the pass, shoots, and crashes the boards.
- Shot is rebounded and passed to corner player on side where the pass originated. Post players then begin another cut or screen.
- 1, 2, and 3 pass the ball among each other. 3, 4, and 5 do the same, which compels the post players to time their cuts and screens so they are always going to meet the ball.

Variation:
- Have the passer also crash the boards on a shot by the post. Then this perimeter player gets the ball, dribbles out to the corner while the other two players slide one position over toward the middle of the court (if 4 made the pass, then he would dribble out to the corner where 5 was while 5 filled 4's original position).

Drill #65: Two-Ball Screening, Passing, and Shooting

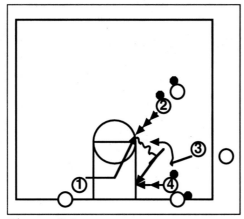

Diagram 5-9

Positions: 1, 2, 3, 4, 5
Number of Players: 8
Time: 2 minutes

Description:
- Players in lines 2 and 4 each have a basketball. 1 flash pivots to high post.
- 2 passes ball to 1. 1 dribble screens for 3. 3 dips away from the screen, and then comes over the top of the screen. 3 jump shoots and rebounds his own shot.
- 1 rolls off his screen. 4 passes ball to 1 for a jump shot or a lay-up.
- 1 rebounds his own shot.
- These screens are not the only two that can be worked in this two-ball screening drill. You can also require moves before players shoot. You can also set the screening drill up at different spots on the floor from day to day. It is best when you use part plays from your own offensive sets.

Rotations: 1 to 2 to 3 to 4 to 1. Each of these rotations are to the ends of each line.

Drill #66: Reading Screens: Curl or Flair

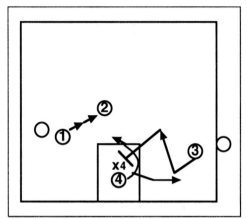

Diagram 5-10

Positions: 1, 2, 3, 4, 5
Number of Players: 7
Time: 2 minutes

Description:

- Line 1 begins with a basketball.
- 1 passes to 2 and makes a V-cut behind 2.
- 3 makes a V-cut toward the ball before going to screen for 4.
- 4 cuts around 3's screen, using either a curl cut or a flair cut. This decision depends upon X4's defensive tactics. 4 must read X4 accurately.
- You can set this screening maneuver up anywhere on the court, not just as shown in Diagram 5-10.

Rotations: 1 to 2 to 3 to 4 to X4 to 1. 4 goes to the end of 1's line and 2 goes to the end of 3's line.

Drill #67: Reading Screens: Screener or Cutter

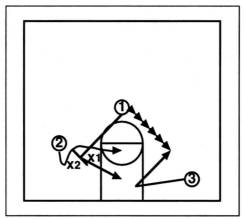

Diagram 5-11

Positions: 1, 2, 3
Number of Players: 5
Time: 3 minutes

Description:
- Line players up as shown in Diagram 5-11.
- 3 dips and V-cuts to receive a pass from 1.
- 1 goes to set the screen for 2. 2 sets up his defender.
- 2 reads the screen and cuts off 1. 1 rolls.
- 3 reads the defenders, X1 and X2, to determine where he should pass.
- The receiver either shoots, drives to the basket, or passes to his teammate for a move, shot, or drive.
- X1 and X2 battle 1 and 2 for the rebound.
- This drill may be run from any location on the court. It should be changed from day to day.

Rotations: 1 to 3 to X1 to X2 to 2 to 1.

Drill #68: Continuous Team Screening

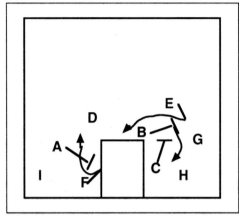

Diagram 5-12

Positions: 1, 2, 3, 4, 5
Number of Players: 9 or more
Time: 1 minute

Description:
- Line entire team up in half-court scoring area (Diagram 5-12).
- Tell players the type of screens you wish to work on for the day. In Diagram 5-12, the team is working on front, back, and screen for the screener.
- Diagram 5-12 depicts A setting a front screen for F, B setting a back screen for E, and C setting a screen for the screener (B).
- All players must move toward the player for whom they are screening. The screener calls the name of the player for whom they are screening. The player accepting the screen dips and cuts around the screen.
- No patterns are set for the screen. Players select at random a teammate where they can set a screen.

Variation:
- Instead of screening, players can use the drill for cutting, or a combination of each. For example, in Diagram 5-12, A sets the screen for F, and then A runs the flair cut before looking to set another screen for another teammate.

Drill #69: Six Basket Alternating Screens

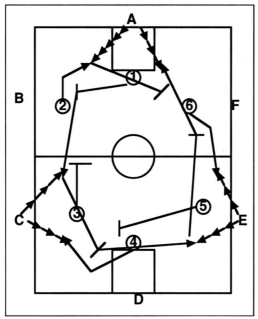

Diagram 5-13

Positions: 1, 2, 3, 4, 5
Number of Players: 12
Time: 2 minutes

Description:

- All six players underneath the basket have basketballs (Diagram 5-13).
- It is easy to remember who sets the next screen: If you set the screen at the previous basket, you are the cutter at the next basket.
- You can require players to run the same screen at each basket (for example, screen and flair). Or you can demand a different screening technique at each basket (for example, at one basket run the screen and flair, and at the next basket screen and roll, and at the next basket a back screen, etc.).
- The rebounder/passer (A, B, C, D, E, F in Diagram 5-13) passes the ball to the cutter. The cutter makes a move and shoots, or the cutter shoots off the screen.
- After one minute, the players running the screens become the rebounders/passers and the rebounders/passers become the new screeners and cutters.
- For ease of explanation, Diagram 5-13 shows 1 in a full trip around the six baskets. All other players would be performing in the same sequence. When you set a screen at one basket, you receive the screen at the next basket.

Drill #70: Continuous Shuffle Screen, Flair Cut Into Dribbling Screen

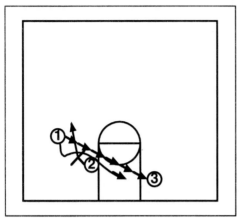

Diagram 5-14

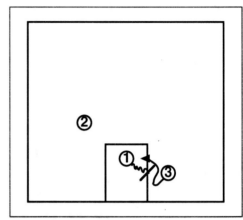

Diagram 5-15

Positions: 1, 2, 3, 4, 5
Number of Players: 3
Time: 1 minute

Description:

- Put three players in a straight line anywhere on the court. Alter starting spots and vary the types of screens set from day to day.
- In Diagram 5-14, 1 passes to 3 and dips to receive a screen from 2. 1 cuts off 2's screen, and 2 flairs.
- 3 passes to 1 coming off 2's screen. 1 immediately runs a dribbling screen for 3 to cut off.
- 1 now passes to 3, who passes to 2, or 1 could keep his dribble alive and pivot pass to 2. The players are now in position to begin the drill again by getting the ball outside to 2.
- 2 begins the drill again by passing to 1 (1 is now where 3 began the drill), and 2 cuts off 3's screen (3 is now where 2 commenced the drill, and 2 is where 1 initiated the drill).

Variation:

- You can allow a move and a shot anywhere along the drill. 1 can take the shot off the shuffle cut, 3 can take the shot off the handoff from the dribbling screen, or either player can pass to 2, who can take the shot off the flair cut. All three crash the offensive boards. The players then realign to continue the drill.

Drill #71: Buddy Screening

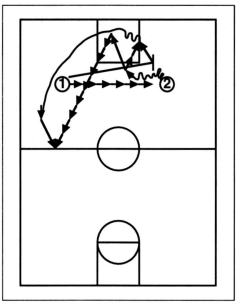

Diagram 5-16

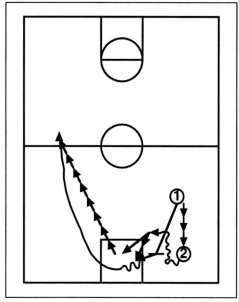

Diagram 5-17

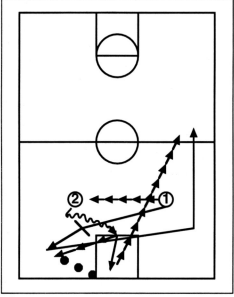

Diagram 5-18

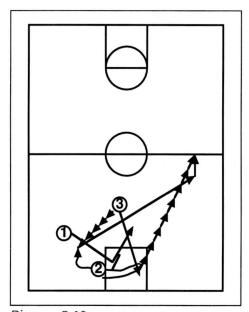

Diagram 5-19

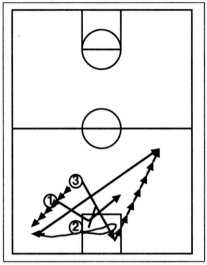

Diagram 5-20

Positions: 1, 2, 3, 4, 5
Number of Players: 2, 3, 4, or 6
Time: 3 minutes

Description:

- All different types of screens can be used. If only two players are being used, then screens on the ball are all you can run. If three players are being used, then screens away from the ball can be run. Defenders can be placed on each attacker and make the drill a live drill, or the drill can be run stressing execution.

- In Diagram 5-16, 1 passes the ball to 2, and 1 goes to set the screen on 2. 2 dribbles around the screen, and 1 rolls to the basket. 2 passes to 1, who shoots the lay-up. 2 rebounds the shot while 1 takes off down the court. 2 outlet passes to 1. 2 sprints to the other end of the court where another screen is executed.

- Diagram 5-17 depicts another angle to set the same screen.

- Diagram 5-18 illustrates 1 setting the screen, and then flaring out for the pass back from 2.

- Diagram 5-19 displays three players with a screen away from the ball.

- Diagram 5-20 shows a screen away from the ball followed by a flair cut.

- Whenever three players are used on offense, you can use only two defenders. These defenders are on the screener and the player using the screen. Doing so not only compels the screener and the receiver to read the defense of the screens, but it requires the passer to read the defense.

- The best sequence of screens to use is the screens in your offense used in the same order as they appear in your offense. You can use the same order as in your secondary break.

6

Cutting

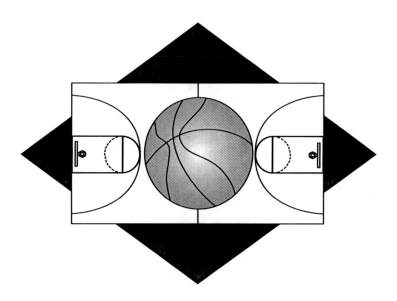

Drill #72: Entire Spectrum Cutting

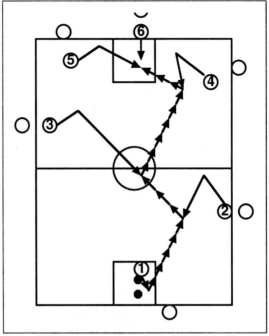

Diagram 6-1

Positions: 1, 2, 3, 4, 5
Number of Players: 12
Time: 3 minutes

Description:

- 1 tosses ball off the board and rebounds it. 1 pivots and throws an overhead outlet pass to 2. 1 must sprint down the sideline outside the perimeter of the court. 1 must get to the 5 position before the pass reaches 4. 1, 5, and 6 are the post positions. The others are perimeter positions.
- 2 starts the fast break. 2 must V-cut down floor and come back to meet the outlet pass.
- 3 simulates the press breaker part of the drill. 3 V-cuts and breaks to the middle of the court for a pass from 2. 3 must catch this pass in back court.
- 4 must get open at the wing to start the half-court offense or to simulate a sideline portion of a fast break or a press breaker. 4 times his cut to the big block area before cutting hard to the wing for a pass from 3. 3 can be dribbling toward 4, or you can require the entire drill to be run without a dribble.

- 5 V-cuts to the high post area. 5 is defended by 6. 5 must read 6. 5 can post-up. 5 can cut backdoor. 5 can receive a pass from 4 and make an offensive move, or 5 can receive a pass from 4 and pass back to 4, who has cut to an open spot (simulating an offensive zone cut) for a jump shot. 6 boxes 5 off the boards regardless of who takes the shot (4 or 5).
- 5 and 6 battle for the offensive boards. If 5 gets the boards, 5 uses a pump fake and a power lay-up. If 6 gets the boards, he must outlet pass to 3. 5 becomes the new 6. 6 sprints outside the court's perimeter to the end of line 1. 6 must get there before the passes because 6 is the new "5" on that end of the court. 1 is the defender.
- Each line receiver must be cutting when the previous line is catching the ball.

Variation:
- Instead of just passing the ball down the floor, you can demand dribbling to get the perfect angle for the next pass.

Rotations:
- 1 to 5
- 2 to 3
- 3 to 4
- 4 to 2
- 5 to 6
- 6 to 1

Drill #73: Fast Break and Half-Court Cutting

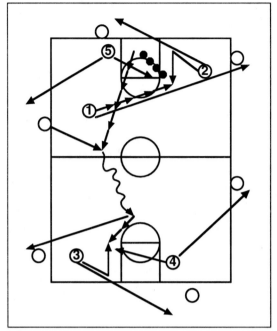

Diagram 6-2

Positions: 1, 2, 3,
Number of Players: 6
Time: 2 minutes

Description:
- 2 V-cuts for a pass from 1. 5 closes out on 2. 2 must read 5's defense. 2 either makes a move or shoots before 5 can get there.
- 2 crashes the boards while 5 boxes out. If 2 gets the rebound, 2 pump fakes and uses a power lay-up.
- If 5 gets the rebound, 5 outlet passes to 1's line. The new 1 must make a cut downcourt and come back to receive the ball.
- 1 now dribbles down to the other end of the court while 3 V-cuts to get open. 4 closes out on 3. The drill continues.

Variation:
- 5 can begin by playing denial defense on 2. 2 must use cuts to free himself from a good denial defense before 1 can get the pass to 2. 4 plays denial defense on 3 at the other end of the court.

Rotations: 1 to 2 to 5 to 1 to 3 to 4 to 1.

Drill #74: Six Simultaneous Cutting

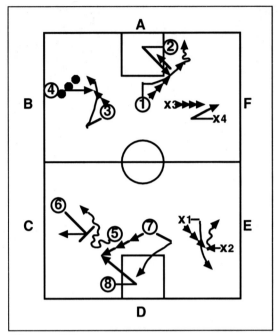

Diagram 6-3

Positions: 1, 2, 3, 4, 5
Number of Players: 2
Time: 3 minutes

Description:

- Place two players at each of six baskets. After running through one of your offensive sets, divide that set into six cutting and shooting maneuvers.
- Have the players perform only one maneuver at each basket. Have them execute this tactic for one half of a minute before rotating to the next basket and the next ploy.
- Have the players rotate during that one half minute so each player will perform at each of the two positions.
- In Diagram 6-3, 1 passes to 2 at basket A, and cuts behind 2 for a handoff. 2 rolls to the basket.
- 3 passes to 4 at basket B, and cuts behind 4 for a jump shot behind the screen.
- 5 fakes away from 6 at basket C. Meanwhile, 6 comes across to set screen for 5. 6 rolls to the basket.
- 7 passes to 8 at basket D, but 7 does not break behind 8. Instead, 7 cuts on a middle cut for a return pass from 8.

- X1 passes to X2 at basket E, and X1 cuts behind X2. X2 fakes handoff and dribbles right for the jump shot.
- X4 is overplayed at basket F, so X4 cuts backdoor for a lob pass from X3.
- As you can see, these plays are partial plays off of an initial cut up the side of the key. You should create any partial play which is a component of your offense.
- You will find that drilling only one partial play at each of the six baskets instead of six partial plays at one basket will help your players remember and execute those six partial plays better.

Variation:

- Use three players instead of two. Doing so allows passing and cutting away from the pass. You could use a post player and two perimeter, or two post players and one perimeter, or three perimeter.

Drill #75: Individual All-Purpose

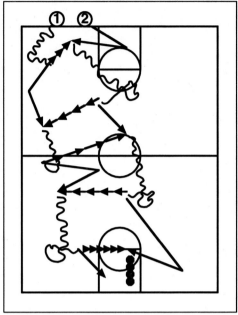

Diagram 6-4

Positions: 1, 2, 3
Number of Players: 2
Time: 1 minute

Description:

- You can divide your squad into pairs. Only one pair is shown in Diagram 6-4 so the explanation will not be cluttered.
- 1 begins with a dribble crossover. 2 meanwhile has V-cut and is yelling to let 1 know where he is. 1 jump stops, pivots, and passes to 2. 2 then dribbles, using a spin move. 1 meanwhile has made a sideline V-cut, yelling to let 2 know where he is.
- 2 passes to 1. 1 begins a dribbling move, in and out, while 2 is running a backdoor cut. This pattern continues down the floor until one player receives a pass within 15 feet of the basket. That player shoots while the other player rebounds, and then they begin the same procedure back down the court.
- If you are using an entire squad, the second set begins when the first set has completed their first move. This situation could get crowded, so the players must communicate with each other.

Drill #76: Perimeter and Post Cutting

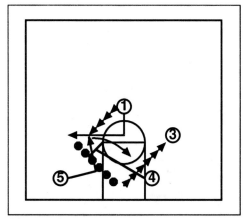

Diagram 6-5

Positions: 1, 2, 3, 4, 5
Number of Players: 4
Time: 2 minutes

Description:
- Line players up as shown in Diagram 6-5.
- 1 starts drill by passing to the cutting 5. 1 cuts off 5's screen for a handoff and jump shot. 1 is purely a point-guard position. Therefore, 1 stays as 1 when rotation occurs. 3, 4, and 5 are wings and posts; therefore, they change positions when rotation occurs.
- 4 rebounds 1's shot. If made, 4 outlet passes to 3. If missed, 4 pump fakes and shoots a power lay-up before outlet passing to 3.

- When 4 passes to 3, 4 screens up for the cutting 5. 5 gets pass from 3, makes an inside move, and shoots. 3 breaks to the basket for rebound position from perimeter after passing to 5. Instead of cutting to the basket, 5 can cut across the lane for a move followed by a jump shot.

Variation:
- Have all players make an individual cut as they move from one line to the next. For example, 3 could flash pivot before moving to the new 4 position. 4 could V-cut while becoming the new 5. 5 could flair cut before becoming the new 3.

Rotations: 1 to 1. 3 to 4 to 5 to 3.

Drill #77: Warm-Up Cutting

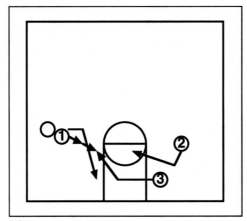

Diagram 6-6

Positions: 1, 2, 3
Number of Players: 4
Time: 2 minutes

Description:
- 1 passes to 3 who has flash pivoted. 1 then executes a backdoor cut.
- Meanwhile 2 executes the middle cut after 1 has passed to 3.
- 3 performs the flash pivot cut, receives a pass from 1, reverse pivots, and either makes a move, shoots, or passes to the cutting 1 or the cutting 2.
- Whichever player receives the pass from 3—either 1 or 2—shoots the lay-up. The other player rebounds and outlet passes to the next player in 1's line.

Variation:
- Put a defender on 1 and a defender on 2. At this point, 1 and 2 must read their defender's defensive positioning to determine if they will make a middle or a backdoor cut. The new rotation would be 1 to 2 to 3 to X1 to X2 to end of 1's line.

Rotations: 1 to 2 to 3 to end of 1's line.

Drill #78: Simulated Half-Court Individual Cutting

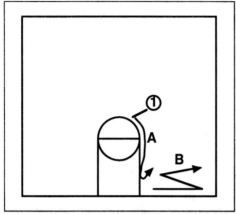

Diagram 6-7

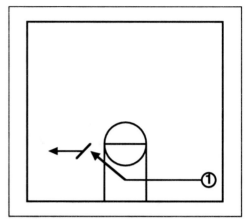

Diagram 6-8

Positions: 1, 2, 3
Number of Players: 1
Time: 30 seconds

Description:
- 1 simulates a pass to a wing teammate (Diagram 6-7). 1 runs a middle or a backdoor cut (A). 1 could run a diagonal cut to the other side of the court, and then flash pivot back toward the wing.
- 1 stops at the low post and tries a few maneuvers to free himself from an imaginary post defender. 1 V-cuts into the corner (B), trying to relieve the conceived denial pressure of a wing or corner defender.
- Diagram 6-8 illustrates a pass being reversed to the opposite side of the court. 1 flash pivots toward the nonexistent ball attacker. 1 then screens for the imaginary wing cutter. 1 runs a flair cut after his screen (could have been a screen and roll, for example).
- 1 continues his cutting calling out which cut he is using and why.
- 1 can even simulate receiving a pass, making a move, passing off, and running yet another set of cuts. 1 continues this movement for 30 seconds.

Variation:
- A defender can be placed on 1. 1 now must make decisions based on what the defense gives.

Drill #79: Dribble, Pass, Pivot, and Cut

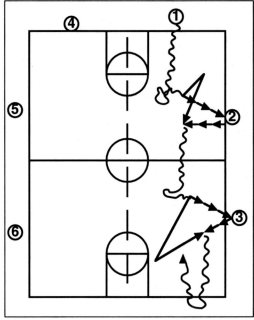

Diagram 6-9

Positions: 1, 2, 3
Number of Players: 3
Time: 1 minute

Description:

- 1 dribbles, making a dribbling move if he wishes, jump stops, pivots (uses either front or reverse), and passes to 2. 1 must stay on one side of the court. You can have other members of the team operating on the other side of the court.
- 1 makes a cut, calling out what he does: middle or backdoor cut, V-cut, or flash pivot, for example.
- 2 passes back to 1.
- 1 dribbles, making a different dribbling maneuver. 1 jump stops, pivots (using either front or reverse), and passes to 3.
- 1 executes a cut, calling out what he does.
- 3 passes back to 1. 1 dribbles to the end line, making yet a third dribbling maneuver before pivoting and beginning a dribble back down the floor.
- 1 should go down the floor and back before the players rotate. You can require 1 to dribble down left-handed and pass right, dribble right-handed and pass with his left hand, dribble right and pass right, and so forth. Have 1 use any combination he needs for improvement.

Variations:

- 1 can set an imaginary screen and run screen-and-roll or screen-and-flair, and so forth.
- A defender can be placed on 1, compelling 1 to make real cuts to take advantage of what the defense offers.

Rotations: 1 to 2 to 3 to 1.

Drill #80: Cutting, Moves, and Shooting (Three Players)

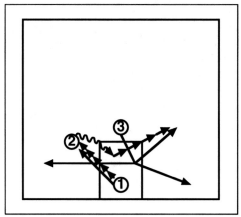

Diagram 6-10

Positions: 1, 2, 3
Number of Players: 3
Time: 3 minutes

Description:
- Put three players at each basket (only one group is shown in Diagram 6-10 for simplicity of explanation).
- 1 passes to 2 and closes out on 2. As 2 drives by 1, 3 either flairs to the right or to the left, requiring 2 to know where his teammate is.
- 2 can stop and take a jump shot. In this case, 3 crashes the offensive boards while 1 chooses to either block out 2 or block out 3.
- 2 can drive and pass off to 3 for 3's jump shot or three-point attempt. In this case, 1 will hurry out on 3 to contest the jump shot. 3 can shoot the jumper, or 3 can drive by the rushing 1 and pass off to 2, who has cut to another spot on the floor. If you are working on three-point shots, 2 would want to cut to a spot behind the three-point arc. Whichever player shoots, both crash the boards while 1 chooses one of the players to block off the boards.

Variations:
- Have 3 take the ball out of bounds, and have 1 deny the entry pass to 2. At this point, 3 cuts to an open three-point spot while 2 drives on 1. The drill continues as previously described.
- When the pass is made from 1 to 2 and 1 closes out on 2, 3 can set a screen, and then roll or flair cut.

Rotations: 1 to 2 to 3 to 1.

Drill #81: Full-Court, Three-Lane Cutting and Passing

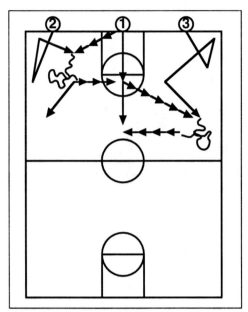

Diagram 6-11

Positions: 1, 2, 3
Number of Players: 3
Time: 1 minute

Description:

- 2 and 3 cut, dribble, and then pass back to 1 all the way down the court and back before rotating.
- 2 and 3 alternate their cuts: V-cut, flash pivot, backdoor, give-and-go, flair, and so on.

Rotations: 1 to 2 to 3 to 1.

Drill #82: Post Open Cuts

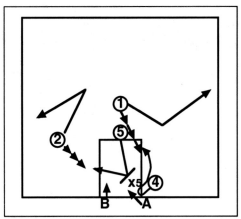

Diagram 6-12

Positions: 4, 5
Number of Players: 7
Time: 5 minutes

Description:
- Line players up as shown in Diagram 6-12. Both 1 and 2 begin with basketballs.
- Any type of cuts to get open can be drilled. However, Diagram 6-12 depicts 5 screening for 4, and 5 keeping X5 on his back to receive a pass from 2 for a move and a shot.
- When 4 receives his pass from 1, 4 can shoot, or make a move and then shoot. Once the shot is taken, 4 crashes the boards and battles A for the rebound. If A gets the rebound, he outlet passes to 1, who has cut to the sideline, for the imaginary fast break. If 4 gets the offensive rebound, 4 pump fakes and shoots a power lay-up.
- When 5 receives his pass from 2, 5 can shoot, or make a move and then shoot. Once the shot is taken, 5 crashes the boards and battles B for the rebound.
- X5 also contests 5 and B for the second rebound. If a defender gets the rebound, he outlet passes to 2 for the imaginary fast break. 2 cuts to the sideline for the outlet pass. If 5 gets an offensive rebound, he pump fakes and shoots a power lay-up.

Rotations:
- 4 to 5 to X5 to A to B to 4
- 1 to 2 to 1.

Drill #83: Multiple Cutting

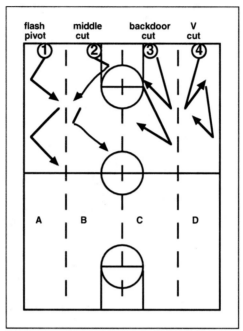

Diagram 6-13

Positions: 1, 2, 3
Number of Players: 4
Time: 2 minutes

Description:
- Line players up as shown in Diagram 6-13.
- Players are to run a specific cut down and back twice before going to the next line.
- Line A runs a flash-pivot cut, line B executes the middle cut, line C performs the backdoor cut, and line D V-cuts in Diagram 6-13. Of course, all the other cuts in your offense can be performed by designating a line for each cut.

Variation:
- You can have the cutter simulate receiving a pass off his cut. The cutter could then perform an offensive move before commencing another cut.

Rotations: 1 to 2 to 3 to 4 to 1

Drill #84: Cutters Off Post

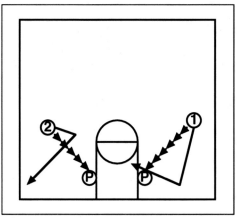

Diagram 6-14

Diagram 6-15

Positions: 1, 2, 3, 4, 5
Number of Players: 2
Time: 2 minutes

Description:
- This drill needs one post player and one perimeter cutter.
- You can work on all the options in your offense which involves a post passer/dribbler and a perimeter cutter.
- You can change positions on the court from day to day so all options will be covered.
- In Diagram 6-14, 1 is shown passing to the post player and dipping before cutting off the post for a jump shot, drive, or drive with a pass back to the post (left side of the court). On the right side of the court, 2 passes to the post player. 2 then fade cuts to the open spot against a zone.
- In Diagram 6-15, 1 passes to the post and begins a V-cut into the corner. Meanwhile the post dribbles and sets a screen for 1. 1 can shoot, drive, or drive and pass back to the post who tries to keep his defender on his back (left side of court). On the right side of the court, 2 passes to the post and fade cuts into the corner, simulating a cut against a zone. The post drives to the basket before passing to 2 in the corner.

Variation:
- If your offense calls for two perimeter cutters off of the post, you can add another perimeter player and practice those three.

Drill #85: Three-Perimeter Cutting and Shooting

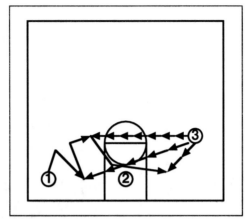

Diagram 6-16

Positions: 1, 2, 3
Number of Players: 3
Time: 3 minutes

Description:

- 2 rebounds and passes to 3. 1 meanwhile has executed a cut and got into position to shoot. 3 passes to 1 for the shot. This process continues until 1 has taken 10 shots, and then the three players rotate.
- You can have 1 work on a single specified cut for the 10 shots, or you can compel 1 to work on 10 different cuts (one for each shot).

Rotations: 1 to 2 to 3 to 1.

7

Rebounding

Drill #86: Quickness Rebounding

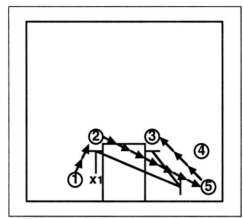

Diagram 7-1

Positions: 1, 2, 3, 4, 5
Number of Players: 6
Time: 3 minutes

Description:
- Line players up in shooting positions around the basket with one of them on defense (Diagram 7-1).
- The ball is passed exactly three times. On the third reception, a shot is taken.
- The defender must go cover each pass. If the defender does not cover a pass, a shot is taken by that receiver.
- When a shot is taken, the shooter and the defender execute offensive and defensive rebounding techniques.
- The rebounder of the shot passes the ball out (outlet pass, if the coach wishes). An offensive rebound can be followed by a pump fake and a power lay-up. The original defender takes the place in the line where the shooter was.
- The shooter becomes the new defender.
- The drill continues following this same procedure.

Variation:
- On the third pass reception, the player can execute a move (either a rocker step or a dribbling move, or both).

Drill #87: Full-Court Rebounding

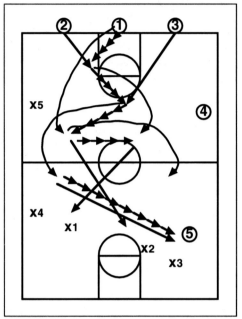

Diagram 7-2

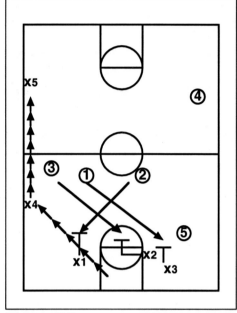

Diagram 7-3

Positions: 1, 2, 3, 4, 5
Number of Players: 8
Time: 3 minutes

Description:

- Three offensive players, 1, 2, and 3, run a weave to half court, or the three offensive players may move at random across the court (anything to make the defenders adjust to pick up the attackers).
- Whoever has the ball as he crosses half court immediately passes to 5.
- 5 makes a move and shoots while 1, 2, and 3 crash the offensive boards.
- X1, X2, and X3 must block 1, 2, and 3 off the boards. They can block out by yelling names out, or they can block out as prescribed by the coach.
- If 1, 2, or 3 gets the rebound, he pump fakes and powers the ball back in the basket. They keep at it as long as they get the offensive rebound.
- When the defenders get the rebound, they outlet pass to X4, who immediately passes to X5.
- X5 makes a fake, including a dribbling move, and shoots. X1, X2, and X3 run in a random manner down the floor (never in a straight line). X1, X2, and X3 go for the offensive rebound, while 1, 2, and 3 must find their assignments and block off the boards.

- If X1, X2, or X3 gets the offensive rebound, he pump fakes and shoots the power lay-up. If 1, 2, or 3 gets a rebound, he outlet passes to 4, who immediately passes to 5. The drill continues.

Variations:
- When a basket is made, the defenders take the ball out of bounds and must pass to a teammate before passing to the sidelines for the fast break. Doing so allows the new defenders to deny the inbounds pass before retreating to play defense beyond the half-court line.
- Have the sideline helpers make cuts before they can receive a pass.

Rotations: After 30 seconds, X4 and X5 replace two of X1, X2, and X3, and 4 and 5 replace two of 1, 2, and 3.

Drill #88: Rebounding Agility

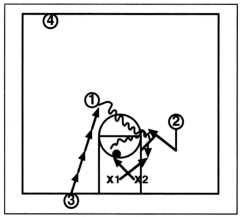

Diagram 7-4

Positions: 1, 2, 3
Number of Players: 4
Time: 2 minutes

Description:
- Coach begins drill by passing ball to 1 or 2 (1 in Diagram 7-4).
- 1 and 2 have option of executing any maneuver they wish (pass-and-screen, pass-and-cut, etc.). In Diagram 7-4, 1 dribble screens for 2. 2 cuts off the screen and shoots a jump shot.
- X1 and X2 remain under the basket until either 1 or 2 shoots.
- Once shot is taken, X1 and X2 must cross each other and block out 1 and 2. 1 and 2 must hit offensive boards hard.
- On an offensive rebound, 1 and 2 pump fake and shoot a power lay-up. On a defensive rebound, X1 and X2 blast out with a dribble.

Variation:
- Have another offensive player (3 in Diagram 7-4) initiate the drill with a pass into either 1 or 2. Have a fourth offensive player (4) around half court. On a defensive rebound, the outlet pass is made to this player at half court. The rotation then is 1 and 2 to X1 and X2 to the player underneath the basket and the player at half court. Those two (the one underneath and the one at half court) become the new 1 and 2.

Rotations:
- 1 to X1 to 1
- 2 to X2 to 2

Drill #89: Offensive Rebounding Footwork

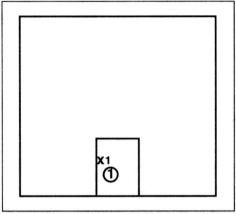

Diagram 7-5

Positions: 1, 2, 3, 4, 5
Number of Players: 2
Time: 2 minutes

Description:
- 1 faces X1. X1 tosses the ball off the board to carom to various spots.
- 1 spins to face the rebound. X1 becomes the defender. When 1 locates the carom, he goes for the rebound or the tip. He must make an instant decision before X1 gets there.
- 1 can use pump fakes, step-throughs, spins, half spins, or any other move you choose to teach as an end-of-the-dribble move or an offensive rebounding move. X1 tries to prevent 1 from scoring.
- After five attempts, X1 and 1 exchange positions.

Variation:
- 1 faces the board, and X1 tosses the ball off the board. X1 spins to block 1 off the boards. 1 uses his offensive steps to get around the box out. You can begin this drill by not using a basketball. In this case, 1 walks through his steps until he has them mastered. In this variation, X1 and 1 exchange positions underneath the boards (not shown in diagram).

Drill #90: Block Out and Outlet Pass

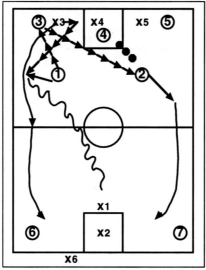

Diagram 7-6

Positions: 1, 2, 3, 4, 5
Number of Players: 13
Time: 4 minutes

Description:
- Offensive players pass the ball around until one of them takes a shot. Defenders slide to play perfect defensive positioning (zone or man).
- In Diagram 7-6, 1 passes to 3, who passes to 2, who then shoots. Offensive and defensive rebounding techniques and steps are put into play (you may use your offensive system, or you can use only three attackers as options).
- X3 rebounds the missed shot, outlet passes to 1, who dribbles into the middle lane (Diagram 7-6). 2, who began his move for a possible outlet pass, recognizes that the shot is rebounded on the far side of the court and goes on the fly pattern.
- After rebounding, X3 sprints to fill the third lane. If you teach blast-out rebounding techniques, X3 can blast out and then throw the outlet pass. This approach requires 1 and 2 to make adjustments. The fast break should be completed against X1 and X2 with X6 waiting to start the next phase of the drill. X4 and X5 become the corner attackers, like 6 and 7 on the far end of the court.
- 3, 4, 5 become defenders for the next wave from the far end of the court. X1 and X2 become the guards on the next wave. X6, 6, and 7 provide the defense (as X3, X4, and X5 did on the far end of the court). 1 and 2 retreat to stop the next wave fast break.
- The drill continues in this fashion for four minutes.

Drill #91: Tipping and Conditioning

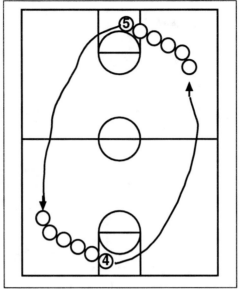

Diagram 7-7

Positions: 1, 2, 3, 4, 5
Number of Players: 12
Time: 2 minutes

Description:

- Divide squad into two groups of six players. Cover the baskets so the players cannot score on their tips. It would also be advantageous if the ricochets would carom in random fashions.
- On signal from the coach, 4 and 5 both toss basketballs into the covered-basket region. Hopefully, the ball will bounce in a different way on each tip, compelling the rebounder/tipper to constantly adjust to make another tip. 4 and 5 immediately sprint to the end of the line on the far ends of the court.
- The second player in each line tips ball toward the covered rims, followed by the third player, the fourth, and so on. After each tip, the player sprints to the other end of the court for a tip there.
- The ball is kept continuously on the rim by tipping it and not allowing it to fall to the floor until two minutes has elapsed. If the ball hits the floor, the drill begins all over again.

- This type of tipping requires agility much as one would see during the game. On one day, have players tip from right side of basket with right hand; on next day have players tip from left side of basket with left hand. You can put a manager on each end of the court with a broom and impel the tipper to tip over the outstretched broom. This drill really requires agility tipping.

Variations:

- You could require players to make a cut while sprinting down the floor. (i.e., a cut to the middle lane to post-up in an effort to break a press).
- You could place a player on each side of the court at the mid-court line with a basketball. This player would pass to the sprinting player, who would pass back on the dead run.
- After receiving the pass, the sprinter could be required to make a dribbling move before passing back.

Drill #92: Scramble Offensive Rebounding

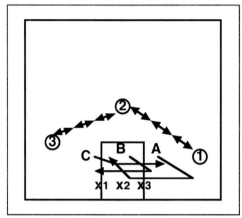

Diagram 7-8

Positions: 1, 2, 3, 4, 5
Number of Players: 9
Time: 3 minutes

Description:
- X1, X2, and X3 are stationed underneath the basket, and cannot move until the shot is taken.
- A, B, and C are running cuts. Make sure they call out which cut they are running.
- 1, 2, and 3 are passing the ball around the perimeter. They can pass as long as they like.
- When either 1, 2, or 3 shoots, X1, X2, and X3 must locate A, B, and C to box them off the boards.
- A, B, and C must avoid the box out and get the offensive rebound. If they get the offensive rebound, they can pump fake and shoot the power lay-up, or tip, or pass back outside to 1, 2, or 3.

Variations:
- In the first step, you can have X1, X2, and X3 face the basket and listen for A, B, and C to call out the shot.
- You can have four players crash the boards, allowing one of them to go untouched to the boards. The defense must significantly adjust when they see the offensive rebound. The four players going to the boards would be A, B, C, and the shooter.
- You can have A, B, and C setting screens for each other.

Rotations: X1, X2, and X3 to 1, 2, and 3 to A, B, and C to X1, X2, and X3.

Drill #93: Outlet Pass, Fast Break, and Conditioning

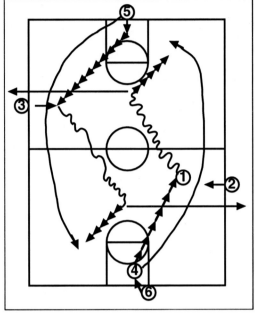

Diagram 7-9

Positions: 1, 2, 3, 4, 5
Number of Players: 7
Time: 3 minutes

Description:

- 4 begins the drill by passing out to 1 (Diagram 7-9).
- 1 dribbles the ball to the middle lane and passes off to the sprinting 4. 1 can pass to 4 around mid-court and get a pass back, or 1 can dribble to the free-throw line and pass to 4.
- 5 rebounds and outlet passes to 3. 1 moves to where 3 had been. 5 must block out the shooter before he can get rebound and outlet passes.
- 3 dribbles the ball to the middle lane and has the same options 1 had in the second step. 5 sprints to become 1's partner on the fast break.
- 6 rebounds and outlet passes to 2. 3 replaces 2. 6 must block out the shooter before he gets rebound and outlet passes.
- The drill continues in this procedure for three minutes.

Variation:

- 5 plays defense on the two fast break players (1 and 4 in Diagram 7-9). Doing so gives a two-on-one fast break. Then both attackers crash the boards as 5 blocks one of them off. 6 would do the same on the other end of the floor, and 4 would execute the defense as 2 and 6 attacks, and so on.

Rotations:

- 1 to 3
- 3 to 1
- 4 to 5
- 5 to 6
- 3 to 2
- 2 to 1.

Drill #94: Six-Basket Offensive Rebounding

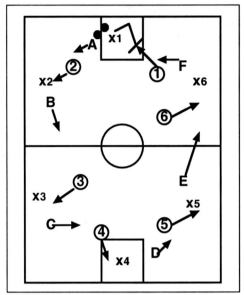

Diagram 7-10

Positions: 1, 2, 3, 4, 5
Number of Players: 18
Time: 2 minutes

Description:
- After shooting, A takes off to the next basket.
- X1 blocks 1 off the boards. X1 will become the next shooter.
- 1 will become the next X1.
- The previous rotation occurs at each basket. The shooter cuts to the next basket, the defender becomes the next shooter, and the attacker becomes the new defender.
- On an offensive rebound, player goes back up with ball. On defensive rebound, the player blasts out with a fast-break dribble to a few steps beyond their shooting position (or you can have the defender blast out, execute a dribbling move, and then return to take the next shot).

Variations:
- This format has unlimited possibilities. For example, 1 can become a cutter with X1 denying him the pass from A. Once he receives the pass, 1 passes back to A, who shoots, and the drill is activated.
- 1 and A can fast break against X1. When the shot is taken, X1 boxes out 1, and the drill continues.

- A can pass to 1. 1 dribble screens for A. A cuts off the screen, gets the pass, and shoots, and the drill begins.

Rotations: Only one basket explained (other baskets do the same). A leaves, X1 becomes A, and 1 becomes X1. If you have fewer than 18 players on your squad, you can eliminate a basket or two.

Drill #95: Rebounding Weave

Diagram 7-11

Positions: 1, 2, 3, 4, 5
Number of Players: 3
Time: 30 seconds

Description:
- 1 and 2 line up on the same side of the board. 3 lines up on the other side (Diagram 7-11).
- 1 tosses the ball off the board to 3's side. 1 immediately moves to a spot behind 3.
- 3 rebounds and tosses the ball back over the basket. 3 immediately moves behind 2.
- 2 rebounds and tosses the ball back over the basket where 1 is now stationed.
- The drill continues in this fashion.

Variation:
- Put a cover over the rim. Use a volleyball. Blow the volleyball up so it is vastly over-inflated, which causes the ball to bounce off the rim erratically. Have the players still run their weave, but have them tip the ball to score. Of course, the ball cannot go in so you have a continuous 30-second tipping drill.

Drill #96: Competitive Rebounding

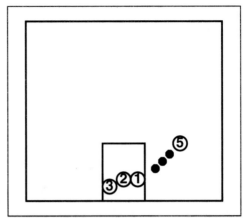

Diagram 7-12

Positions: 1, 2, 3, 4, 5
Number of Players: 4
Time: 3 minutes

Description:
- 5 shoots the ball, and 1, 2, and 3 try to tip the ball into the basket (or one of them will rebound, pump fake, and try to score a basket).
- The rebounder may use up-and-under moves as well. The two defenders may bump the shooter slightly.
- The first player to score five baskets exchanges places with 5. The scoring begins again (or you may allow the players to keep the number they have already scored).
- No dribbling.
- Any ball rebounded outside the lane must be returned to the shooter (5 in Diagram 7-12).
- When a basket is made, the ball is returned to the shooter (or you can allow the rebounder/scorer to keep scoring as long as he can retrieve the made shot and put it back into the basket. This approach would encourage physical play, which you want out of your rebounders).
- 5 could pass the ball to either 1, 2, or 3, and allow him to shoot.

Variation:
- After each made basket, the scorer passes the ball to 5 and makes a cut to another perimeter shooting spot. The other two rebounders also make a V-cut or a flash-pivot cut. 5 passes the ball to the scorer, and 5 and the two non-scorers become the three rebounders as the ex-scorer shoots the jump shot.

Rotations: Player scoring five baskets becomes 5, and 5 becomes one of the three rebounders.

Drill #97: Six-Basket Tip and One-on-One

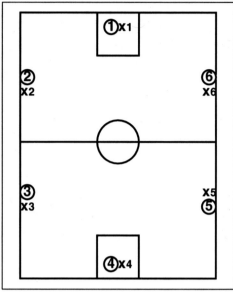

Diagram 7-13

Positions: 1, 2, 3, 4, 5
Number of Players: 12
Time: 6 minutes

Description:

- Put two players at each basket. In Diagram 7-13, only one basket will be discussed, as all the others do the same.
- 1 and X1 alternate tossing the ball off the boards. Both battle hard for the tip in. The player who actually scores becomes the offensive player and the other the defender.
- The attacker must dribble drive to the mid-court circle and then attack the basket where he just rebounded the ball while the defender tries to stop him.
- After one minute, rotate to the next basket.

8

Warm-Ups

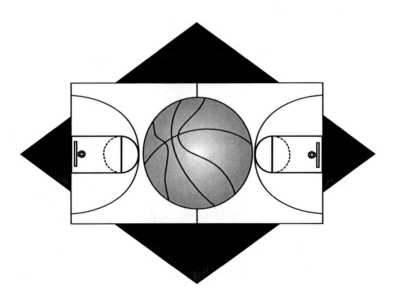

Drill #98: Pressure Scoring

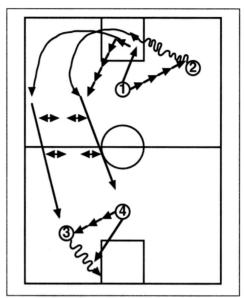

Diagram 8-1

Positions: 1, 2, 3, 4, 5
Number of Players: 4
Time: 2 minutes

Description:

- 1 passes to 2. 2 makes a dribbling move (spin, crossover, etc.) and drives to the basket for a lay-up (or he could shoot a jump shot). Only 1 and 2's side of the court will be explained as 3 and 4 will do exactly as 1 and 2.
- 1 times 2's shooting effort and places his hand in position to slap the shot away, even if he fouls the shooter slightly. 1 could also push 2 slightly to try to throw off 2's shot. This drill is an effort to teach the shooter—especially on lay-ups—to protect the ball from a potential slap from the defender.
- Player switches lines on the far end of the court after each shot.
- On the trip down to the far end of the court, the players pass the ball as they sprint.

Variations:

- 2 must make a V-cut (or a flash-pivot cut or a flair cut) before 1 passes him the ball.
- 1 defends 2 down the court in a dribbling one-on-one drill.

Rotations:

- 1 to 3
- 2 to 4
- 3 to 1
- 4 to 2

Drill #99: Four-Line Dribbling and Shooting

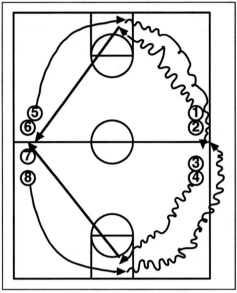

Diagram 8-2

Positions: 1, 2, 3, 4, 5
Number of Players: 8
Time: 2 minutes

Description:

- 1 and 4 drive for lay-ups. They then go to the end of the line on the other side of the court, facing opposite their drives.
- 5 rebounds 1's shot and dribbles to spot behind 3. This move should be a dribbling move (spin, half spin, etc.). 8 rebounds 4's shot and dribbles to the spot behind 2.
- Start the drill on one side of the court one day, and on the other side the next day.
- Instead of driving for a lay-up as shown in Diagram 8-2, players can dribble drive (using a move), stop, and shoot a jump shot.
- Player can also be required to make two or three dribbling moves.
- Lines can start at the three-point arc and begin with a rocker-step series before shooting or driving.

Drill #100: Fundamental Gauntlet

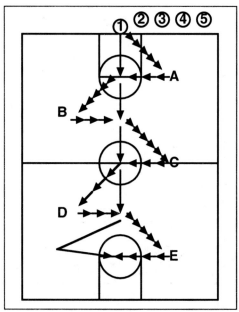

Diagram 8-3

Positions: 1, 2, 3, 4, 5
Number of Players: 10
Time: 2 minutes

Description:
- Line players up as shown in Diagram 8-3. 1, 2, 3, 4, and 5 start with a basketball. This drill can be used to drill on all fundamentals, but only passing will be discussed in this section.
- 1 passes to A and sprints down the floor. A passes back to 1, who quickly passes to B, and continues in this manner down the court. All passes and passing techniques can be covered.
- When 1 passes to E, 1 cuts away and comes back to the ball (V) for a jump shot. 1 rebounds his own shot.
- After 1 has passed to B, 2 begins with his pass to A.
- After 1, 2, 3, 4, and 5 have gone down the floor, they begin in the same order from the other side of the court.
- 1, 2, 3, 4, and 5 pass through and jump shoot for one minute before they rotate with A, B, C, D, and E.

Variations:

- Instead of passing, 1 can dribble to the next player, stop, pivot, and then pass.
- Instead of passing, 1 can perform different dribbling moves down the floor by driving up to A, perform a maneuver, then drive to B.
- Instead of passing, 1 can pass, go set the screen for the lettered player, then roll and get a pass back, or the lettered player can set a screen for the numbered player, and fades, flairs, and so forth can be used.
- Instead of passing and sprinting, 1 passes and runs a cut before he gets a pass back.
- Instead of passing, 1 is defended by A until 1 gets near B. At the point where A and B come together, they double-team 1. 1 must keep his dribble alive. When 1 breaks this double-team, 1 continues dribbling with B defending until they get near C. At this point, B and C double-team 1, which continues until 1 approaches E. Then E and 1 go one-on-one.
- All fundamentals can be drilled using this format.

Drill #101: Recovery and Pivoting

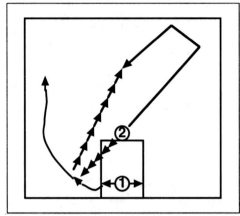

Diagram 8-4

Positions: 1, 2, 3, 4, 5
Number of Players: 2
Time: 1 minute

Description:
- Divide squad into groups of two.
- In Diagram 8-4, 1 is facing out of bounds, and looking away from 2.
- 1 is sliding from one side of the free-throw lane to the other. When 2 yells, "Now," 1 jump stops and pivots to face the ball. Meanwhile 2 has rolled the ball or passed it somewhere near 1. 1 must locate the ball and recover it. 1 then makes a quick move (dribbling move) down the floor as if to fast break. 1 then passes the ball to 2. 1 sprints back into place again facing the baseline, looking away from 2 and begin sliding again.
- 1 slides for 30 seconds before rotating with 2.

Variations:
- Instead of making a dribbling move, 2 can cut off 1, using 1's screen to get a pass and a jump shot.
- Instead of making a dribbling move, 1 can quickly face the basket, make a rocker-step move, and shoot. 2 can block off 1 as they battle for the rebound.
- 2 cuts to an open perimeter spot after he passes. 1 must find him for a quick pass and jump shot. 1 can box 2 off the boards in a rebound battle.
- 2 cuts to a spot on the floor (middle lane) for 1 to quickly locate, pass to, and break down the sideline for a pass back, simulating breaking a press. This variation is shown in Diagram 8-4.
- All fundamentals can be drilled using this format.

Drill #102: Extreme Pressure Lay-Up

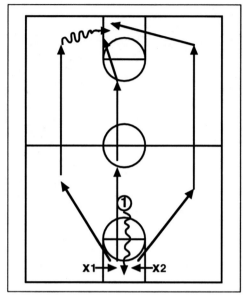

Diagram 8-5

Positions: 1, 2, 3
Number of Players: 3
Time: 1 1/2 minutes

Description:
- 1 drives hard for a lay-up.
- X1 and X2 slide into the lane on both sides of 1. X1 and X2 try to strip 1 of the ball as 1 tries to lay-up the shot.
- X1 and X2 may slightly bump 1 if they cannot deflect or steal the ball.
- 1 must learn to protect the ball against two defenders while shooting a lay-up.
- If X1 or X2 steal the ball, they fast break against 1 to other end of the court. If X1 or X2 rebounds, they fast break to other end of the court. When they get to free-throw line extended, one of those two must attack the basket with a dribble. The other two try to strip the ball, and then they rotate.
- If 1 misses the shot, he battles for the offensive rebound.

Variation:
- Instead of fast breaking with the ball, whichever player recovers the ball (either by steal or rebound) goes one-on-one against the other player (between X1 and X2).

Rotations: 1 to X1 to X2 to 1.

Drill #103: Two-Ball Warm-Up and Shooting

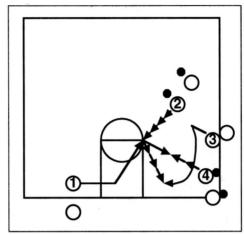

Diagram 8-6

Positions: 1, 2, 3, 4, 5
Number of Players: 8
Time: 4 minutes

Description:
- Players in lines 2 and 4 each have a basketball (Diagram 8-6).
- 1 flash pivots to high post.
- 2 passes ball to 1. 3 cuts backdoor for a pass from 1 and a lay-up. 3 rebounds 2's shot.
- 1 curls to side post for a pass from 4 and a jump shot.
- 1 rebounds 4's shot.

Variation:
- You can set up two sequential shots off of your half-court set offense or two consecutive shots off your secondary break.

Rotations:
- 1 to end of 2's line
- 2 to end of 3's line
- 3 to end of 4's line
- 4 to end of 1's line

Drill #104: Multiple Purpose Warm-Up

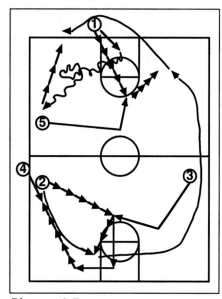

Diagram 8-7

Positions: 1, 2, 3, 4, 5
Number of Players: 5
Time: 2 minutes

Description:
- 2 passes to 3 and makes a cut for a lay-up or a jump shot (Diagram 8-7). 3 can even make a cut before receiving a pass.
- 2 can use a move (either dribbling or rocker step) before shooting a lay-up, or 2 can use a move at the end of the dribble around the basket.
- 3 rebounds the shot and passes to 4, who has used a cut to receive the pass, which can be an outlet pass for fast break, or a post-up in the middle of the court for breaking the press (or a sideline cut, if you prefer the sideline attack to break presses).
- Meanwhile, 2 sprints to the opposite end of the court. 5 makes a middle-lane post cut to break the press. 5 receives a pass from 1 to simulate breaking the press. When 5 receives the pass, he passes to 2 who can make a dribbling move for a jump shot or a lay-up. 1 rebounds 2's shot and dribbles to the sideline mid-court area, using a dribbling move, replacing 5's vacated spot. 1 now passes to 2 and the drill continues.

Variation:
- You can have 5 set a dribbling screen for 2 on the last phase of the drill, or 2 can set a screen for 5 to dribble around and run your screen-and-roll.

Rotations: 1 to 5 to 3 to 2 (behind 4 in the line) to 1.

Drill #105: Dribbling Moves Warm-Up

Diagram 8-8

Positions: 1, 2, 3
Number of Players: 2
Time: 1 minute

Description:
- 1 executes a rocker-step fake, and then 1 performs a dribbling move.
- 1 shoots at the end of his dribbling maneuver. 1 battles 2 for the offensive rebound. 2 comes from weakside and tries to block 1 off the offensive boards.
- If 1 rebounds, 1 pump fakes and shoots a power lay-up. When 2 gets the rebound, 2 dribble drives to the corner where he runs a spin move.

Variation:
- 1 passes to 2. 1 makes a cut (V or fade or flash-pivot, etc). 2 passes to 1, and 1 executes the rocker fake, followed by hen the dribbling fake, and then the shot. The drill continues.

Rotations: 1 to 2 to 1.

Drill #106: Recovery and Break

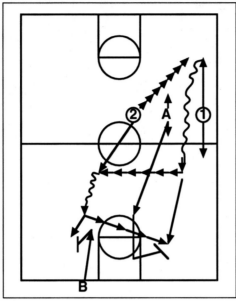

Diagram 8-9

Positions: 1, 2, 3, 4, 5
Number of Players: 4
Time: 2 minutes

Description:

- 1 cuts to get away from A, who is playing between 2 and 1. 2 rolls the ball so A must move to recover it. A can gamble for it if he thinks he can get it first.
- 1 and 2 fast break against A.
- When 1 and 2 get into scoring range, the one with the ball uses a dribbling maneuver before he takes a shot. 1 takes the shot in Diagram 8-9, but 2 could be the player who takes the shot.
- B steps onto the court and boxes out 2 in Diagram 8-9.
- If the shot is missed, 1 and 2 crash the offensive boards while A and B block them off the boards.
- If 1 or 2 gets the boards, he pump fakes and then shoots a power lay-up. If A or B gets the boards, the two will fast break to the other end of the court against 1 and 2. If the shot is made, A and B throw the ball in bounds and bring the ball up the court against 1 and 2.

Variation:

- Instead of shooting the ball off of a move, 1 sets a dribbling screen for 2 to break around. 2 then shoots the ball, and the drill continues.

Rotations:

- 1 and 2 become A and B
- A and B become 1 and 2

Drill #107: Half-Court Screening and Cutting

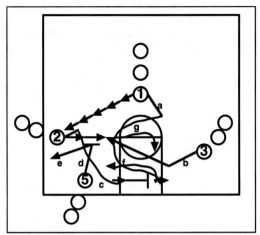

Diagram 8-10

Positions: 1, 2, 3, 4, 5
Number of Players: 12
Time: 2 minutes

Description:
- Line players up in the four positions represented by 1, 2, 3, and 5 (Diagram 8-10).
- The players perform the cuts are discussed designated by the letters in the diagram.
- First, 1 passes to 2 and executes the give-and-go, the middle cut, or the backdoor cut, stopping at the big block weakside (a).
- 3 flash pivots (b), receiving a pass from 2.
- Meanwhile, 5 has set the back screen (c) for 2 to cut around (d).
- 5 flairs to the wing (e), getting the pass from 3.
- 2 continues his cut (f), setting a cross screen for 1 (f).
- 3 goes backdoor for lob pass from 5.
- 5 has option of using a move and shooting a jump shot, pass to 1 on the cut off 2's screen, or toss a lob pass to 3.

Variation:
- You can break down your half-court offense regarding its cuts and screen and use those cuts and screens as a warm-up drill.

Rotations: Players rotate to end of each line: 1 to 2 to 5 to 3 to 1.

Drill #108: Fly-Pattern Outlet Passes

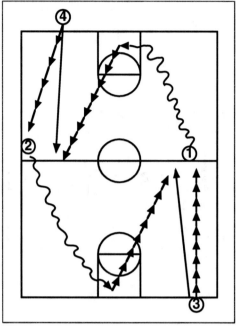

Diagram 8-11

Positions: 1, 2, 3, 4, 5
Number of Players: 4
Time: 2 minutes

Description:
- 3 and 4 begin with basketballs and pass to 1 and 2 respectively (Diagram 8-11).
- 1 and 2 drive for lay-ups.
- 1 and 2 rebound their own shots. 3 and 4 break up the sidelines. 3 and 4 begin their break as 1 and 2 begin their actual lay-up motion.
- 1 and 2 pass to 3 and 4, who dribble drive for the lay-up.
- Drill continues in this fashion for two minutes.

Variations:
- Instead of players running the sideline fly pattern, the players sprint down the sideline to about half-court before cutting back into the middle lane for a post-up pass (simulating breaking the full-court press). When the passer passes to the middle-lane player, the passer sprints up the sideline for a pass back.
- Instead of driving hard to the basket for a lay-up, the player uses a dribbling move or two and stops to shoot the jump shot.

Drill #109: Heaven or Hell

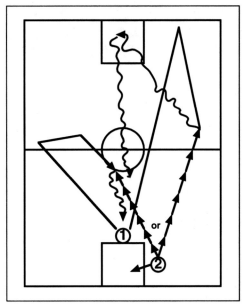

Diagram 8-12

Positions: 1, 2, 3, 4, 5
Number of Players: 2
Time: 2 minutes

Description:

- Partners line up to shoot two free throws (or two jumps shots).
- Rebounder works on offensive rebounding (steps if you teach them, and pump fakes and power lay-ups if the shot is missed).
- Both players shoot two warm-up free throws. Then each player begins his heaven-or-hell shots. Heaven means you get to throw the passes; hell means you must do the running.
- When heaven or hell commences, the shooter must make both free throws. If he misses one of the two, the shooter sprints to half-court, cuts back into the middle lane for a pass and a press-break simulation; if he misses both free throws, the shooter sprints to the other end line. On his sprint to other end line, the player catches the pass, makes a speed dribble for a lay-up, and then returns to the original free-throw line with a speed dribble.
- The shooter must make the next free throw or he is off again on a sprint to half-court or full-court (he goes the same distance as he did initially). This pattern continues until he makes the free throw, and then the drill begins again.

Variation:

- Instead of catching a pass and making a driving lay-up, the sprinter catches the pass, makes a dribbling move, and shoots a jump shot.

9

Fast Break

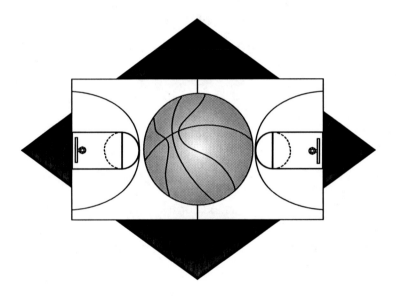

Drill #110: Multiple Fast-Break Passing

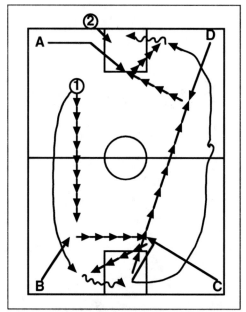

Diagram 9-1

Positions: 1, 2, 3, 4, 5
Number of Players: 6
Time: 3 minutes

Description:
- Line players up as shown in Diagram 9-1.
- 1 starts the drill by throwing a baseball or overhead outlet pass to the cutting B. 1 sprints hard as he releases the pass.
- Upon B receiving the pass, C cuts to the foul line extended. B passes to C.
- C pivots and passes to the cutting 1. 1 shoots a lay-up. C follows his pass to 1 for the rebound. 1 goes to the B position. C throws a baseball or overhead outlet pass to D.
- Upon D receiving the pass, A cuts up other side of lane. D passes to A. A bounce passes to C for the lay-up.
- 2 rebounds and passes to A. A assumes 1's initial role, and the drill continues.

Rotations: 1 to B to C to D to 2 to A to 1.

Drill #111: Four-on-Four-on-Four

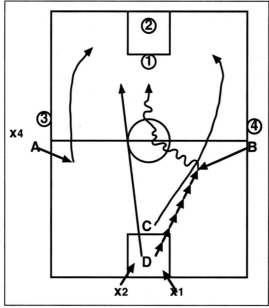

Diagram 9-2

Positions: 1, 2, 3, 4, 5
Number of Players: 12
Time: 5 minutes

Description:

- Divide the 12 players into three squads of four: A, B, C, D; 1, 2, 3, 4; and X1, X2, X3, X4. Line the players up as shown in Diagram 9-2.
- All squads have two players at half-court to receive outlet passes.
- The rebounder (or throw-in player, if a point is scored) is the trailer in a four-on-two fast break.
- Players rotate so they play each position.
- Keep score by going to 30, with two points for each score and one point for each stop by the defense.
- In Diagram 9-2, D rebounds and outlet passes to B. B dribbles to the middle of the court while A takes the left lane and C takes the right lane. D trails. X1 and X2 step onto the court as the tandem defenders when 1, 2, 3, and 4 bring the ball back down the floor.

- 1 and 2 play tandem defense against A, B, C, and D's fast break. Whoever rebounds the missed shot or throws the made shot in becomes the trailer as 1, 2, 3, and 4 attack X1 and X2.
- The drill continues until 30 points are scored.

Variation:

- You can make it a four-on-three or a four-on-one fast break by having one of the next outlet pass receivers become a defender (four-on-three) or by taking away one of the tandem defenders (four-on-one).

Drill #112: Three-on-Two-on-One

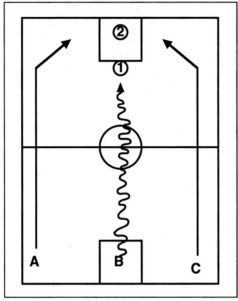

Diagram 9-3

Positions: 1, 2, 3, 4, 5
Number of Players: 5
Time: 2 minutes

Description:

- A, B, and C attack 1 and 2 in a three-on-two fast break.
- A, B, and C can pass ball down the floor instead of using a dribble.
- A, B, and C can run a three-man weave instead of passing or dribbling, or they can combine passing, weaving, and dribbling.
- Whoever takes the shot (among A, B, and C) returns back down the floor as the lone defender as 1 and 2 fast break in a two-on-one matrix. The other two (of A, B, and C) stay as the next tandem defenders when 1, 2, and the shooter of A, B, and C fast break back down the floor against the two who did not shoot in a three-on-two fast break.
- If either A, B, or C throw the ball away, then the player throwing the ball away would race back down the floor as the lone defender in the two-on-one fast break.

Drill #113: Three-on-Three-on-Three

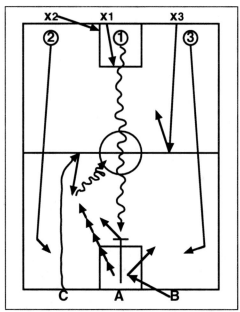

Diagram 9-4

Positions: 1, 2, 3, 4, 5
Number of Players: 9
Time: 4 minutes

Description:
- Line players up as shown in Diagram 9-4.
- 1, 2, and 3 attack A and B in a two-on-one fast break format. C sprints up to half-court as the three-on-two break ends.
- If a shot is missed, 1, 2, and 3 crash the boards against A and B. C can come back to help block out the third attacker.
- If the shot is missed and a defender gets the rebound, the rebounder outlet passes to C. A, B, and C then attack X1 and X2 on the far end of the court in a three-on-two fast break. X3 would sprint to half-court as the three-on-two break ends. X3 would come back for the outlet pass and a continuous fast-break format.
- This pattern continues for four minutes.

Variation:
- C can stay underneath the basket on the first wave of the fast break by 1, 2, and 3. C steps onto the court, and the teams play a three-on-three motion-type half-court drill until a scored point, or a missed shot and an outlet pass.

Drill #114: Fast Break and Press Breaker

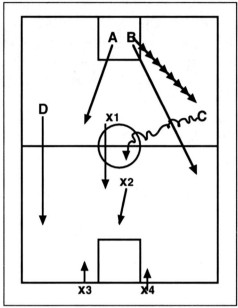

Diagram 9-5

Positions: 1, 2, 3, 4, 5
Number of Players: 8
Time: 6 minutes

Description:
- A, B, C, and D are the offensive players; X1, X2, X3, and X4 represent the defenders. After three minutes, the squads exchange positions.
- A tosses the ball off of the board. B rebounds it. On the next possession, B should toss the ball off the boards for A to rebound it.
- B outlet passes to C. B can blast out with a dribble before passing to C, if that is part of your philosophy on fast breaks.
- C dribbles the ball to the middle lane while D fills one lane and B fills the other lane in a three-on-two fast break. The two defenders, X1 and X2, can play parallel or tandem defense. A becomes the trailer in a four-on-two fast break.
- If A, B, C, or D score, the drill is set up from the scoring end, and the defenders race to opposite end of court. If a shot is missed, the players battle for the offensive rebound. If X1 or X2 manage to get the defensive rebound, he fast breaks against the shooter in a two-on-one situation (or you can demand the drill begin anew from the original defensive end).

- If X1 or X2 can create a turnover, those two fast break against the player who turned the ball over in a two-on-one fast break.
- X3 and X4 can be allowed to step onto the court to make the fast break four-on-three (just X3 on the court), or four-on-four with both X3 and X4 on the court.
- If a point is scored, A, B, C, or D take the ball out of bounds. X3 and X4 face guard the first two receivers. They can even be allowed to double-team the inbounds receiver. X1 and X2 gamble for interceptions as A, B, C, and D work the ball up the court against the press.
- The drill is a fast break down the court and a press breaker back up the court. After three minutes, the other squad gets a chance to become fast-break players and press breakers.

Drill #115: Three-on-Three Call

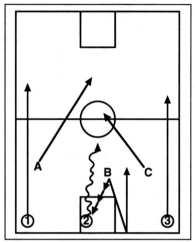

Diagram 9-6

Positions: 1, 2, 3, 4, 5
Number of Players: 6
Time: 4 minutes

Description:

- B passes the ball to 2 in Diagram 9-6. B can pass the ball to any of the three attackers.
- This pass compels B to go touch the baseline before he can rejoin A and C on defense. Doing so gives a three-on-two fast break unless B can hustle back into the fray, making it a three-on-three fast break. If B had passed the ball to 3, for example, then C would have had to touch the baseline before reentering the defense.
- 1, 2, and 3 fast break against A and C, knowing that B is hustling back into defense. A and C try to delay the fast break until B can recover.
- A, B, and C stay on offense for the trip back down the floor. The squads then exchange positions.

Variations:

- Add another attacker and another defender, making the drill a four-on-four fast break.
- Have the pass always go to the corner offensive positions (either 1 or 3) and have the defender on that side and B double-team the receiver. The opposite defender plays safety in an attempt to steal the outlet pass, or delay the new receiver's dribbling advance after breaking the press. This double-teaming pressure can continue all the way down the floor, or an immediate fast break can occur on any completed outlet pass.

Drill #116: Three Drill Offensively

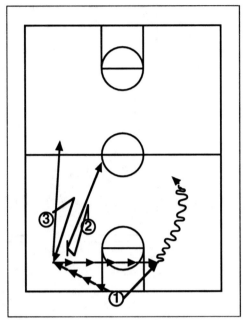

Diagram 9-7

Positions: 1, 2, 3
Number of Players: 3
Time: 3 minutes

Description:
- 1 and 3 attack 2 in a two-on-one full-court fast-break and press-breaker drill.
- In Diagram 9-7, 1 passes to 3 as 2 tries to prevent the inbounds pass. 3 receives the pass and passes quickly back to 1. 2 retreats to try to stop the two-on-one fast break.
- You can require 1, 2, and 3 to bring the ball down floor in a dribbling or passing weave before the press begins.
- You can mandate 1 and 3 to pass the ball up the floor against 2's defense. Doing so would compel constantly cutting to get free from 2 to receive a pass.

Rotations: 1 to 2 to 3 to 1.

Drill #117: Post Fast Break

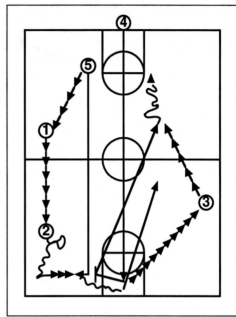

Diagram 9-8

Positions: 4, 5
Number of Players: 5 (all post-type players)
Time: 5 minutes

Description:
- Diagram 9-8 displays 5 passing to 1, who quickly passes to 2.
- 5 sprints for post-up position on 4.
- 2 dribbles until he gets passing angle into 5. 5 goes one-on-one inside against 4.
- 5 and 4 battle for rebound on a missed shot. On a made shot, 4 takes the ball out of bounds and passes to 3.
- On a missed shot, if 4 gets the rebound, he outlet passes to 3. 4 goes on a dead sprint, simulating trying to get ahead of the defense on a fast break. 3 leads 4, who dribbles to the basket for a lay-up. 5 sprints to try to stop 4's attack.
- 4 and 5 exchange places, the drill continues for one minute, and then the rotation begins

Variations:
- Instead of having 4 play defense on 5, 4 can be the trailer in the fast break. 4 stops at the head of the circle and receives a pass from 2. 4 then dumps down to 5, who makes a move and scores. When using this variation, 5 would then get the rebound, outlet pass to 3, and 5 becomes the trailer. 4 would post-up low and get the dump-down pass from 5. The variation would continue using this procedure.

Rotations: 1 to 2 to 3 to 4 to 5 to 1.

Drill #118: Three-on-Two to Three-on-Two

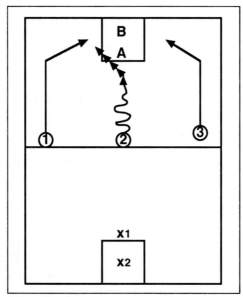

Diagram 9-9

Positions: 1, 2, 3
Number of Players: 7
Time: 4 minutes

Description:
- 1, 2, and 3 fast break against A and B (Diagram 9-9).
- Whoever takes the shot (or turns the ball over) teams up with A and B for a three-on-two fast break to the other end of the court against X1 and X2.
- The two who did not take the shot (or turn the ball over) stay on defense. For example, if 2 takes the shot (or turns the ball over), 2, A, and B would fast break against X1 and X2. If B takes the shot (or turns the ball over) in the latter three-on-two fast break, then B, X1, and X2 would fast break against 1 and 3 (who stay on defense on the other end). This same process continues for four minutes.

Variation:
- If one player needs the conditioning (or the extra fast-break work), you should designate that player to always be on offense.

Drill #119: Recovery and Transition Circle

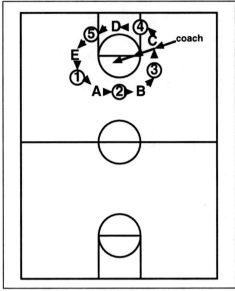

Diagram 9-10

Positions: 1, 2, 3, 4, 5
Number of Players: 10
Time: 1 minute

Description:
- Line up two teams of five players at the foul circle in close proximity. Alternate players from the two teams so that one player from one team is always between two players of the other team.
- Players begin sliding around the circle at reasonable speed.
- The coach has a ball. The coach can shoot the ball (all 10 players crash the boards), roll ball between two players (a big scramble should result for the recovery), toss the ball into middle of the revolving circle (10 players should be after it), or pass directly to one player. This approach allows the coach to make sure that both teams get fast-break transition work.
- The team who recovers the ball is on offense, and they attack to the far end of the court. Defensive team must quickly organize and get back on defense.

Variation:
- Have all 10 players execute specific cuts at half-court level. For example, players may flash pivot, V-cut, or screen-and-fade cut. Others cuts or screens can be worked on at the next practice. No one is on defense. Coach throws ball into the middle of the pack. Team that recovers is on offense, and they fast break to the far end of the court.

Drill #120: Fast-Break Outlet and Baseball Passing

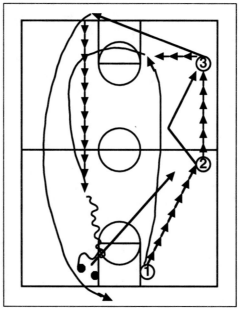

Diagram 9-11

Positions: 1, 2, 3, 4, 5
Number of Players: 3
Time: 2 minutes

Description:
- Line the three players up as shown in Diagram 9-11.
- 1 begins the drill with a toss off the boards followed by an outlet pass (or blast out if you have it in your fast-break system). 1 sprints the length of the court.
- 2 passes to 3. 3 bounce passes to the sprinting 1. 1 drives for the lay-up, and 3 follows for the rebound.
- 1 does not stop. He sprints hard to the other end of the floor.
- 3 rebounds, steps out of bounds, and tosses a long, leading baseball pass to 1. 3 follows 1 down the floor.
- 1 makes a dribble move and shoots a jump shot. 3 rebounds and outlet passes to 1, who has replaced 2. 2 has replaced 3, and 3 has assumed the duties of 1. The drill continues.

Variation:
- You can require 2 and 3 to make cuts before they receive the passes.

Rotations: 1 to 2 to 3 to 1.

Drill #121: Team Fast Break Into Three-on-Two-on-One

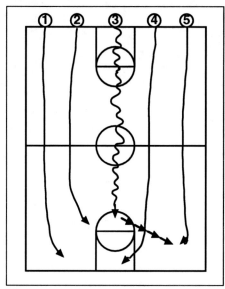

Diagram 9-12

Positions: 1, 2, 3, 4, 5
Number of Players: 5
Time: 2 minutes

Description:

- Begin with five players on baseline running the floor using your form fast break. The team can run the secondary break before the shot is taken (not shown in Diagram 9-12).
- Player who passes the ball to the shooter and the shooter race back down the floor to play defense against the other three players in a three-on-two fast break (in Diagram 9-12, 3 and 5 would become the defenders).
- 3 and 5 race back to play defense on 1, 2, and 4.
- Whoever shoots the ball between 1, 2, and 4 would become the defender in a two-on-one fast break against the two defenders (3 and 5 in Diagram 9-12).
- The lone defender, when the break is over, dribbles the ball back down the floor to the original starting positions using different dribbling moves. The drill continues.

Variation:

- Instead of a three-on-two break, it could be a two-on-three full-court pressure defense. In this case, the passer and the shooter take the ball out of bounds and try to advance it against the other three players, who would be using full-court pressure, including double-teaming traps.

Drill #122: One-on-One Into Five-on-Five

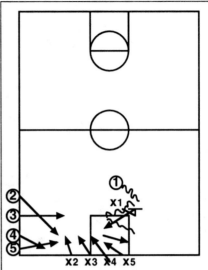

Diagram 9-13

Positions: 1, 2, 3, 4, 5
Number of Players: 10
Time: 10 minutes

Description:

- 1 goes live in a one-on-one drill against X1. Next possession, 2 goes live in a one-on-one drill against X2.
- On shot, X1 boxes out 1. 2, 3, 4, and 5 scramble onto the court as 1 releases the shot. X2, X3, X4, and X5 race onto the court, trying to box out 2, 3, 4, and 5. 2, 3, 4, and 5 can cross or do any maneuver to complicate and confuse X2, X3, X4, and X5.
- On rebound by the defenders, they fast break to the other end of the court. They can run the secondary break, or set up their half-court offense, or both. This break can be a form break, or 2, 3, 4, 5, and 1 can play defense.
- On a made shot by 1, the defenders run fast break after a made shot. This break can be a form break, or the ex-attackers can be defenders.
- After the break, successful or not, 2 goes onto the floor to play one-on-one against X2. The drill continues.
- After five minutes, the teams exchange duties.

Variations:

- Instead of one-on-one, the players can go two-on-two into five-on-five, or three-on-three into five-on-five. When running two-on-two or three-on-three, you can require players to use partial plays from your offensive system, or you can allow freelance play.
- Instead of fast break after made basket, you can have the defenders turn attackers run your press breakers. This drill can either be a form drill, or you can make it live versus the ex-offensive players turned defenders.

Drill #123: Phases of the Fast Break

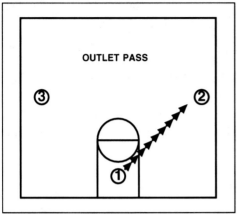

Diagram 9-14

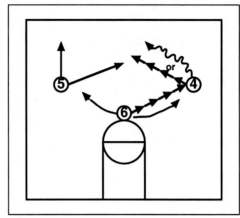

Diagram 9-15

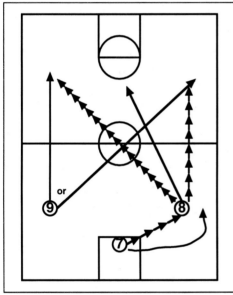

Diagram 9-16

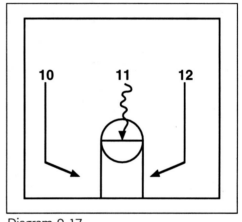

Diagram 9-17

Positions: 1, 2, 3, 4, 5
Number of Players: 12
Time: 4 minutes

Description:

- The phases are broken into four categories: outlet pass (Diagram 9-14), middle-lane cutting (Diagram 9-15), fly pattern (Diagram 9-16), and end of break (Diagram 9-17).

- Each phase is practiced separately by three players. After one minute, the players rotate to the next phase. You can practice all four phases at one time during a practice, or do only one phase at a time for four different segments of your practice schedule.
- Diagram 9-14 displays the initial phase. 1 tosses the ball off the boards, rebounds, pivots, and outlet passes to 2 or 3. 1 could blast out if that's part of your philosophy of the break. After 20 seconds, the three players rotate near one of the baskets.
- This phase occurs around mid-court (Diagram 9-15), and it is called middle-lane cutting. 6 reads 4, and 5 and cuts accordingly. 6 tosses the ball to either 4 or 5 (in Diagram 9-15, the toss is to 4). 4 decides to either dribble the ball to the middle-court lane or pass to 5, who has cut to the middle lane. 4 reads 5's cut to make his decision. 6 goes down 5's outside lane if 5 cuts to the middle. Otherwise, 6 cuts down 4's lane. Players rotate after each cut.
- The third phase, demonstrated in Diagram 9-16, must occur on a second court, which can easily be done in most gymnasiums by having all the drilling occur at the two side courts. 8 passes to 9, who went on a fly pattern. 7 goes on a fly pattern down 9's original outside lane. Players rotate after each fly pattern.
- Diagram 9-17 illustrates the end of the break sequence. It is a simple three-on-zero fast-break drill. You can make it more by requiring a move at the end of the pass before a shot is taken, or you can have players break behind screens (pass and follow), or pass and screen away, or pass and cut. Players rotate each spot after each shot is taken.

Press Break

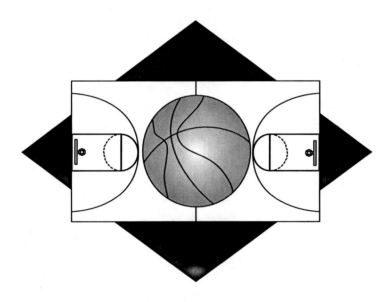

Drill #124: Full-Speed Passing and Press Breaking

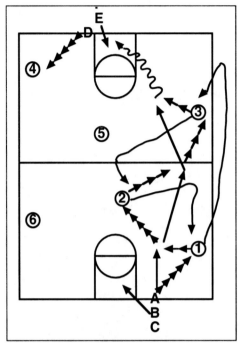

Diagram 10-1

Positions: 1, 2, 3, 4, 5
Number of Players: 12
Time: 4 minutes

Description:
- Line 12 players up as shown in Diagram 10-1: six passers and six drivers. A and D begin with a ball. They start their first pass at the same time: A down the right sideline, and D down the left sideline.
- A passes to 1 and sprints, getting a pass back from 1. A immediately passes to 2, who has cut into the middle lane and posted up. A continues his sprint up the sideline. 2 passes back to A. Meanwhile, 3 has cut into a sideline posting position. A passes to 3. 3 passes back to A. A now has the option to drive hard for the lay-up, make a dribbling move and drive hard for the lay-up, or make a dribbling move and take a jump shot.
- D is performing the same tasks down the opposite sideline as A was executing down the right sideline. D's route is not pictured in Diagram 10-1 for simplicity of explanation.
- E rebounds A's shot. E begins the same procedure down the other sideline. B rebounds D's shot and the drill continues down both sidelines.

- After 1 receives his pass and passes back to A, 1 sprints down the sideline and comes back to meet B's pass. After 2 has passed to A, 2 V-cuts in a sideline posting pattern. After 3 has passed to A, 3 runs a flash-pivot cut into a strong middle-lane posting position for a pass from B. 1, 2, and 3 time their cuts just as they would if they were running a press offense. 1, 2, and 3 should be exchanging positions constantly (as should 4, 5, and 6 on the other side of the court).
- The passers and the drivers exchange positions after two minutes.

Variations:
- You can have the drivers make dribbling moves after they receive each pass.
- You can have the passers and the drivers run the cuts of your press offense.
- You can allow E to defend A's move to score (B would be defending D on the other side).

Drill #125: Continuous Passing Out of Traps

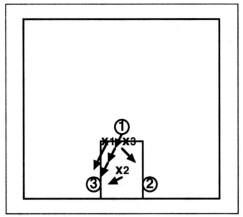

Diagram 10-2

Positions: 1, 2, 3, 4, 5
Number of Players: 6
Time: 2 minutes

Description:
- 1 locates at the free-throw line. 2 is on one big block, and 3 is on the other. All three attackers must stay close to these positions, forcing the passer to fake pass, to accurately access the defender's position, and to throw the necessary pass (bounce or chest or lob) that assures success.
- X1 and X3 trap 1. X2 plays between 2 and 3, hoping to read 1 and deflect 1's pass.
- In Diagram 10-2, 1 has passed to 3 (he could have passed to 2). At this point, X2 and X1 trap 3, and X3 sets up between 1 and 2, reading 3, and gambling for a deflection on 3's pass.
- When the defenders have deflected three passes, they rotate to offense, and the attackers become defenders.

Variations:
- You can allow any successful receiver to dribble drive for a few steps. Doing so compels the defenders to quickly adjust for another trap. When you allow dribbling, the new attackers without the ball must realign themselves at an angle 12 feet or so away from the dribbler.
- You can require the pass receivers to make V-cuts, flash-pivot cuts, and so forth to get into position to receive passes.

Drill #126: Avoid the Flick

Diagram 10-3

Positions: 1, 2, 3
Number of Players: 2
Time: 1 minute

Description:

- 1 begins by dribbling down the floor using a speed dribble one time, and a control dribble the next time. 1 may use dribbling moves (crossover, spin, half spin, etc) if the coach desires. 1 can be limited to one third or one half of the court lengthwise (for example, 1 would have to stay on the left side of the court with an imaginary line from free-throw-lane line to free-throw-lane line, as shown in Diagram 10-3), or 1 can use the entire court.
- X1 trails 1 but tries to flick the ball should 1 ever put ball on same side as X1. X1 can fake going to one side, and then go to the other.
- If X1 flicks the dribble, then X1 and 1 chase the ball. The one who recovers the ball is on offense, the other is on defense in a one-on-one game. X1 would take the ball back to the basket where the drill began. 1, if he recovers it, would continue down the floor. If X1 has not flicked the ball by the time 1 has advanced to the free-throw line extended, X1 must recover into proper defensive positioning to stop 1's drive for a basket.
- When ball is scored by either player, they exchange positions and the drill continues.

Drill #127: Five Drill Defensively

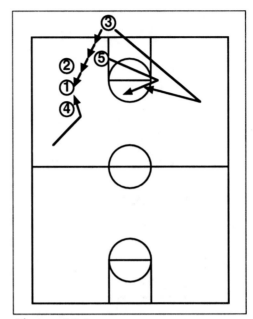

Diagram 10-4

Positions: 1, 2, 3, 4, 5
Number of Players: 5
Time: 3 minutes

Description:
- Five players are used for this drill: three on defense, two on offense (Diagram 10-4).
- 3 tries to pass ball into 1, who is being double-teamed. 5 pressures 3's inbounds pass.
- In Diagram 10-4, 3 passes into 1, and 2 and 4 double-team 1. 1 can try to break the trap with a dribble, or 1 can pass to 3 when 3 frees himself from 5's pressure.
- 3 dips and cuts while 5 tries to prevent the pass back to 3. Should 1 get the pass back to 3, 5 and 3 can go one-on-one, or 2 or 4 can come help 5 double-team 3. 1 would then dip and cut, trying to free himself for the pass back from 3.
- Should a steal occur, it becomes a three-on-two fast break.
- Should 1 and 3 get the ball into a scoring area, they play two against three until they get a good shot.

Variation:
- Instead of double-teaming the receiver, you can designate one player (4 in Diagram 10-4) as a free safety while 2 plays 1 and 5 plays 3. 4 would then gamble for steals on errant passes, or 4 could double-team the dribbler if either 1 or 3 tried to break the press with a dribble.

Rotations: 1 to 2 to 3 to 4 to 5 to 1.

Drill #128: Five Drill Offensively

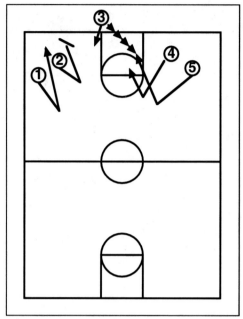

Diagram 10-5

Positions: 1, 2, 3, 4, 5
Number of Players: 5
Time: 3 minutes

Description:

- Five drill offensively: three offensive players and two defenders (Diagram 10-5).
- 3 tries to pass ball into 1 or 5. 2 defends 1, and 4 guards 5. The defenders may use any technique—face guard, denial, or pressure—once the ball enters.
- Once ball is in bounds, 1, 3, and 5 work the ball upcourt against 2 and 4. 2 and 4 can use any defensive strategy.
- When ball is advanced into scoring area, 1, 3, and 5 attempt to score, including offensive rebounding.
- Should 2 or 4 steal a pass or get a defensive rebound, they fast break (or advance the ball against three defenders in a press breaker).

Rotations: 1 to 2 to 3 to 4 to 5 to 1.

Drill #129: Three-Versus-Five Press Breaker

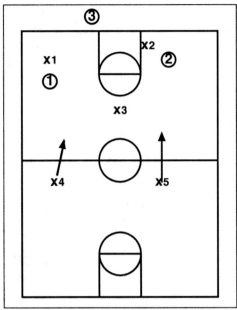

Diagram 10-6

Positions: 1, 2, 3, 4, 5
Number of Players: 8
Time: 5 minutes

Description:
- Line up three attackers (1, 2, 3 in Diagram 10-6), and five defenders.
- The three attackers are to get the ball inbounds against three defenders (X1, X2, and X3). You can put X3 on the inbounds passer, let X3 double-team one of the potential inbounds receivers, or let X3 play center field.
- X4 and X5 cannot come across half-court until the ball is inbounds.
- You can designate X4, for example, to double-team all pass receivers on left side of the court, and X5 to play rover for interceptions. X5 would double-team all pass receivers on the right side, and X4 would play interceptor. This approach gives the defense a zone-press look.
- You could have X4 and X5 drop toward the basket and trap only at half-court level, demonstrating a half-court zone-trap look.
- 1, 2, and 3 must learn to keep their dribble alive, to make proper cuts to open spaces, and to reverse the ball as they attack full- and half-court zone (and man) presses.
- 1, 2, and 3 keep working until they shoot, throw the ball away, or get an offensive rebound (pump fake and put ball back up).
- The defenders fast break on turnovers and on defensive rebounds.

Rotations: 1 to 2 to 3 to X1 to X2 to X3 to X4 to X5 to 1.

Drill #130: Two-Player Posting and Outside Lane Cut

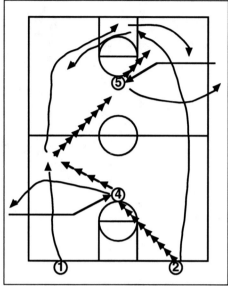

Diagram 10-7

Positions: 1, 2, 3, 4, 5
Number of Players: 4
Time: 2 minutes

Description:
- 2 passes to 4, who pivots and passes to the sprinting 1. 2 goes on a full sprint.
- Both 4 and 5 time their cuts into the middle lane to post-up so 1 and 2 will not have to break their sprint speed. 1 passes to 5, who pivots and passes to 2 for a lay-up. 2 must really sprint hard to get there for the lay-up without the ball hitting the floor.
- 1 rebounds, again without allowing the ball to hit the floor, which requires an all-out sprint by 1. 1 immediately passes to 5, and 2 sprints down other side of court for a pass from 5. 4 begins his cut so 2 will not have to break his sprint.
- 2 passes to 4. 4 pivots and hits 1 for the lay-up. 2 rebounds and the drill continues for 30 seconds before 1 and 2 replace 4 and 5. 4 and 5 become the new 1 and 2 for 30 seconds.
- 1 and 2 must dribble the ball or walk should 4 or 5 not time their cuts correctly, but the drill should be run without the ball ever touching the floor.

Variation:
- 1 and 2, instead of shooting a lay-up, make a dribbling move and shoot a jump shot.

Rotations:
- 1 and 2 become 4 and 5 after 30 seconds.
- 4 and 5 become 1 and 2.

Drill #131: Two-Line Full-Court Beat the Press

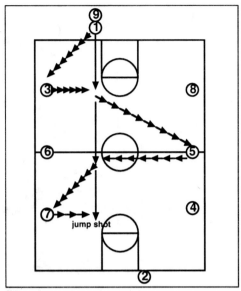

Diagram 10-8

Positions: 1, 2, 3, 4, 5
Number of Players: 9
Time: 3 minutes

Description:
- Line players up as shown in Diagram 10-8.
- Only one side of the court is shown for explanation purposes, but both sides of the court are in operation at the same time.
- 1 passes to 3, who passes back to 1. 1 passes crosscourt to 5. 5 passes back to 1. 1 passes to 7. 7 passes back to 1, who shoots a jump shot. 1 rebounds his shot, passes to 4, and begins his movement down the other side of the court. 2 has already gone down that side of the court. The only difference is when 2 takes his shot, 9 rebounds and begins his movement down the same side as 1 did. Doing so gives 2 (and 1 and 9 when they reach this stage) a moment to get his breath before beginning again.
- Each set of players run their spots for one minute before rotation occurs.

Variations:
- The shooter dribbles and makes a move before shooting.
- The receivers of the passes make a cut before receiving a pass.

Rotations: After 1 minute, 1, 2, and 9 to 3, 6, and 7 to 4, 5, and 8 to 1, 2, and 9.

Drill #132: Avoid the Herd

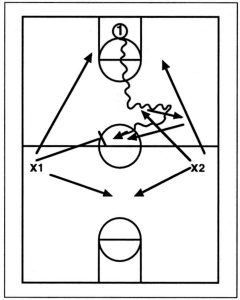

Diagram 10-9

Positions: 1, 2, 3
Number of Players: 3
Time: 1 1/2 minutes

Description:

- 1 begins his dribble from just in front of the basket. X1 and X2 begin just above the half-court line (see Diagram 10-9). X1 and X2 can attack 1 anytime they choose. 1 must be alert and try to dribble around or through the two defenders.
- X1 and X2 can double-team the dribbler. X2, for example, can try to control 1, with X1 timing his move to take the most advantageous positioning against 1. X1 and X2 can play a tandem defense before trapping near half-court. X1 and X2 have free reign to run any type of pressure defense they wish.
- After 30 seconds, the players rotate.

Rotations: 1 to X1 to X2 to 1.

Drill #133: Breaking Pressure by Passing and Cutting

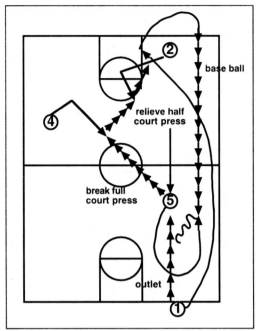

Diagram 10-10

Positions: 1, 2, 3, 4, 5
Number of Players: 4
Time: 2 minutes

Description:
- This drill covers every possible pass and cut involved in breaking presses.
- 1 begins the drill by tossing the ball off the boards and throwing an outlet pass to 5. 5 has sprinted from beyond half-court to a proper sideline position of an outlet pass (or a press breaking sideline pass).
- 5 pivots and passes an overhead pass to the posting 4. 4 has cut from the weakside into the middle lane. 4 pivots and passes to 2.
- 2 cuts to a spot above the free-throw circle in an effort to break half-court zone pressure.
- 1 has cut down the outside lane. 1 must be alert because 5 or 4 can pass to him if it is their wish (not shown in Diagram 10-10). But these passes from either 5 or 4 are often used to break presses. If 1 does receive a pass from either 5 or 4, 1 makes the next pass (for example, if 5 passes to 1, then 1 passes to 4; if 4 passes to 1, then 1 passes to 2). This situation requires both 4 and 2 to adjust their cuts. Most of the time, the passes should occur as shown in Diagram 10-10, with 2 making the final pass to 1 for the lay-up (or an offensive move at the end).

- When 1 shoots, 1 rebounds (made or missed). 1 takes the ball out of bounds and throws a baseball pass to 5. 5 makes a cut up the sideline to receive the baseball pass, simulating breaking the press with a baseball sideline pass. 5 then makes a dribbling move, shoots, and rebounds the ball while 4, 2, and 1 get in position for 5 to begin the drill again.

Rotations:
- 1 to 2
- 2 to 4
- 4 to 5
- 5 to 1

Drill #134: Continuous Press Breaker

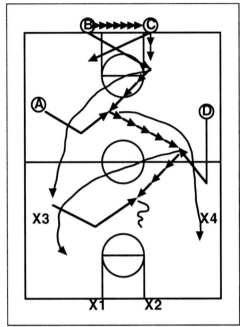

Diagram 10-11

Positions: 1, 2, 3, 4, 5
Number of Players: 8
Time: 4 minutes

Description:

- B passes to C and diagonally cuts for an inbounds pass from C.
- A flash-pivot cuts. B passes to A. B cuts behind A. C trails the entire length of the court, serving as a release or reverse passing option.
- D races downcourt, and then flash-pivot cuts for the pass from A. A cuts behind D.
- Meanwhile, B has raced ahead of D. B flash-pivot cuts for the pass from D.
- D cuts behind B, which results in a three-lane fast break.
- Any middle-lane posting player can dribble drive on any reception. The other attackers must read and be ready to fill the three lanes for a fast break.
- Any middle-lane posting player can reverse the pass to the cutting teammate at any time. Doing so requires the attacker who reverses the ball to cut behind the next post attacker in the outside lane.
- Any middle-lane posting attacker can reverse the ball to the trailing C. This player becomes the trailer while C assumes the cutting maneuvers of the player who passes to C.

- X1, X2, X3, and X4 bring the ball back down the floor, executing as A, B, C, and D did.
- The players rotate as described so all players can play each position.

Variations:
- Put X1 and X2 out in the key area to play defense on the three-lane fast break.
- Run the drill as a sideline press breaker by having the receivers flash back up sideline lane or cut to the opposite sideline lane.
- Run as a fast-break drill by having B and C begin with a defensive rebound.

Rotations:
- A to B to C to D to A
- X1 to X2 to X3 to X4 to X1

Drill #135: Phases of the Press Breaker

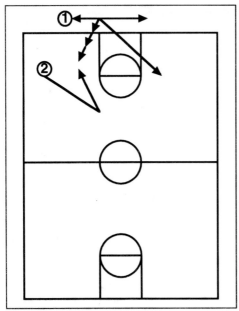

Diagram 10-12

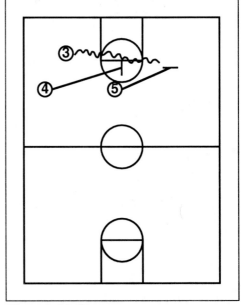

Diagram 10-13

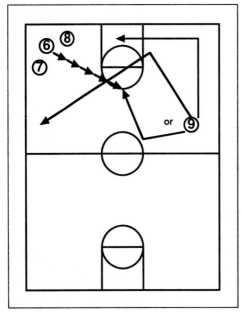

Diagram 10-14

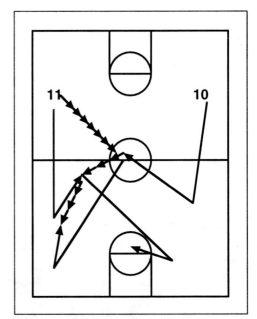

Diagram 10-15

Positions: 1, 2, 3, 4, 5
Number of Players: 11
Time: 4 minutes

Description:

- The drill is run in four phases. Each phase has a diagram to explain it. Players stay in their phase for one minute before beginning the second phase, then the third, and then the fourth.

- In Phase 1 (Diagram 10-12), 2 cuts to get open from an imaginary defender. 1 inbounds the pass and cuts. 2 then takes the ball out of bounds while 1 cuts to get open. (You can also use a third player and give both 2 and the third player a ball. In that case, the drill begins with 1 using peripheral vision to receive alternating timed passes from both in bounds players. The drill then continues with the cuts and inbounds passes previously described.)

- Diagram 10-13 shows Phase 2. 3 begins with a basketball and he has his dribble live. 3 tries to escape the double-teaming efforts of 4 and 5. 3 must never allow the trap to be successful. 3 can dribble retreat in order to get around one side of the defenders, if need be. 3 stops and picks up his dribble once he crosses the half-court line, and then the other two defenders close in on 3. 3 now works on his step-through moves while the other two defenders try to tip the ball away from 3. 3 pivots and swings the ball low, keeping the ball away from either 4 or 5, using his body as a shield. 3 rotates to 4, who rotates to 5.

- Four players are used in Phase 3 (Diagram 10-14). 6 has lost his dribble. 7 and 8 trap 6. 6 can use step-through moves. 9 locates at different spots on the floor. 6 must throw three successful passes to 9 before rotating. 9 works on the cuts of the offense. This drill is begun at different spots on the floor from day to day, so players will have no difficulty regardless of where they pick up their dribble. Players rotate 6 to 7 to 8 to 9.

- Phase 4 is depicted in Diagram 10-15. In this phase, players should work on the cuts in the press offense. In Diagram 10-15, 11 passes to the posting 10. 11 then cuts up the sideline. 10 passes to 11 and runs a diagonal cut. 11 passes to 10 and cuts diagonally away from the ball before flash pivoting back into the middle lane. The drill continues. You can start this drill from anywhere on the court from day to day. 10 rotates to 11 who rotates to 10.

Variation:

- Devote only one minute per day to this drill. All players run the same drill during that minute. After four days, you will have drilled on the four phases of your press offense.

11

Half-Court Offense

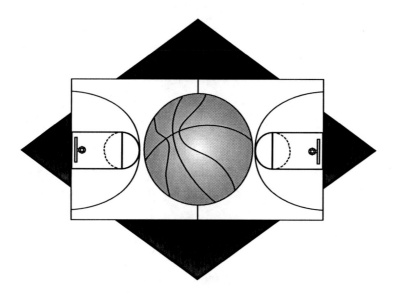

Drill #136: Recognizing Defenses

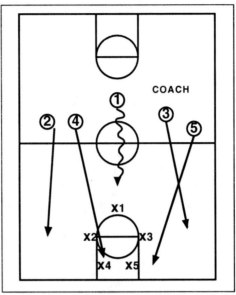

Diagram 11-1

Positions: 1, 2, 3, 4, 5
Number of Players: 10
Time: 6 minutes

Description:
- 1, 2, 3, 4, and 5 bring ball up court to face defense of X1, X2, X3, X4, and X5.
- Coach stands behind the offense and signals to defense which defense they are to run.
- Defense can:
  - ✓ Man one possession, and then zone the next
  - ✓ Play a combination defense (triangle-and-two, etc)
  - ✓ Half-court trap out of man or zone
  - ✓ Man for the first pass, and then run a zone
  - ✓ Zone for the first pass, and then run man
  - ✓ Man if ball is entered on one side of the court, zone if ball is entered on the other side of the court.
- Let the players attack what they think they see until they shoot. Then the coach can correct any bad judgments.

Rotations: After three minutes, offense becomes defense, and defense goes to offense.

Drill #137: Shooting Out of Zone Shell Game

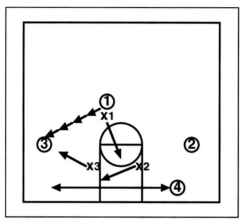

Diagram 11-2

Positions: 1, 2, 3, 4, 5
Number of Players: 7
Time: 3 minutes

Description:

- Diagram 11-2 illustrates a point guard front with two wings and a player running the baseline. The next day you should begin with a two-guard front, a wing, and a player running the baseline. The next day, use a different formation, but always use one more attacker than the number of available defenders.
- 1 passes to 3. X3 covers 3 while the other two defenders get ready to cover the next pass. 3 can pass to 4, skip pass to 2, or reverse pass to 1. Do not assign the defenders specific areas or players to cover. If two defenders go after the same attacker, that attacker should recognize and pass off.
- When an attacker receives a pass and is wide open, that attacker shoots a three-point shot. The four attackers crash the offensive boards against the three defenders. Offensive rebounding should be a major part of your offensive strategy against zones.

Variations:

- You can allow dribble penetration and passing off the drive for shots from the perimeter.
- You can allow cutting by the passers after they make a pass.
- You can permit cutting away from the ball.
- You can use screening if screening is part of your zone offense.
- You could use three attackers against two defenders.

- You could use your five attackers against four defenders, and run your zone offense.
- You could require the defense to stop the offense two consecutive times before rotation occurs.
- You can assign defenders areas to cover.

Rotations:
- 1 to 2 to 3 to 4 to 1
- X1 to X2 to X3 to X1
- After one minute, the three defenders replace three attackers. Those three attackers become the three defenders.

Drill #138: Avoid the Double Down

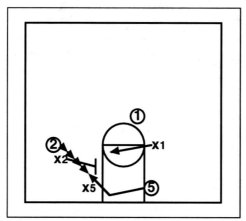

Diagram 11-3

Positions: 1, 2, 3, 4, 5
Number of Players: 6
Time: 4 minutes

Description:
- 1 and 2 pass the ball while 5 tries to free himself from X5 in a live post drill. 1 and 2 can cut or dribble to get proper position.
- Once a pass enters the post, the passer's defender (X2 in Diagram 11-3) doubles down to help X5 defend 5. You could always use the weakside defender as the double-down player.
- 1 and 2 flair cut to perimeter areas, where X1 will have a hard time covering them should 5 pass the ball back out to either 1 or 2.
- 5 passes to either 1 or 2 for a jump shot. Should X1 recover and prevent the jump shot, then another pass is made for the jump shot. If X2 recovers to prevent that shot, the drill continues with 5 working to get open again.
- When a shot is taken, X1, X2, and X5 block out 1, 2, and 5 in an offensive rebounding drill.
- Should the defense get the rebound or a turnover, they fast break.
- Should the offense score, they quickly convert to defense and deny the inbounds pass.

Rotations: From offense (1, 2, 5) to defense (X1, X2, X5) to offense.

Drill #139: Combination Passing, Cutting, Screening, and Shooting

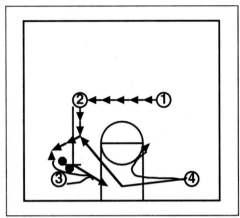

Diagram 11-4

Positions: 1, 2, 3, 4, 5
Number of Players: 4
Time: 3 minutes

Description:
- 4 (or 3) flash pivots or curls. If 4 flash pivots, 2 must have the ball. If 4 runs a curl, 1 must have the ball. 1 and 2 can pass the ball to make sure the correct player has the ball.
- The ball is passed to 4 by 2 in Diagram 11-4.
- On one day, the player who passes to 4 must go set the screen. On the next day, the passer receives the screen.
- In Diagram 11-4, 2 passes to 4 and sets the screen for 3. 3 dips and comes off the screen for the jump shot. All players crash the offensive boards.
- The offense does not have to be run from this array. Use the perimeter format of your offense (for example, run a 1-3 if your offensive set is the 1-3-1).
- Work on single phases of the offense at a time by running that partial play for one minute, then another partial play for a minute, and a third partial play for the third minute.

Variations:
- Put four defenders on the floor and make it a live shell game.
- Allow the defense to fast break on turnovers or defensive rebounds.

- Compel the defense to quickly switch to offense and get the ball in (should the attackers score).
- Instead of working on passing, cutting, screening, and shooting, you can work on any combination you wish.

Rotations: Rotate the players so each will play the actual positions they will play in a ballgame.

Drill #140: Execution of Set Offense

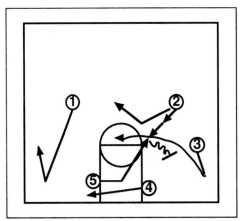

Diagram 11-5

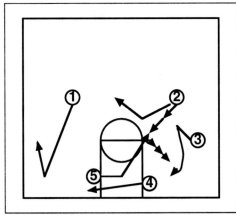

Diagram 11-6

Positions: 1, 2, 3, 4, 5
Number of Players: 5
Time: 5 minutes

Description:

- Half-court offensive options depend on proper reads of defenders. Diagrams 11-5 and 11-6 illustrate 3 reading X3 and executing the proper move. You should use your set offense, break it down to every scoring opportunity, and drill singularly on that scoring opportunity.
- 2 passes to 5 in Diagram 11-5.
- 3 checks X3's coverage. If X3 is even with or below 3's line to 5, 3 will dip. and then cut off 5's dribbling screen. If X3 is above the imaginary line between 3 and 5, 3 will step toward 5, and then cut backdoor for a pass and a lay-up.
- When beginning to teach proper execution, you may add an X3 to provide dummy (and then live) defense. Doing so enables the attacker to readily see and exercise the proper option.

Rotations: Make sure all players play the position they will play during a ballgame. No other rotation should be used.

Drill #141: Half-Court Perimeter Offense

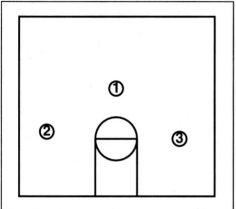

Diagram 11-7

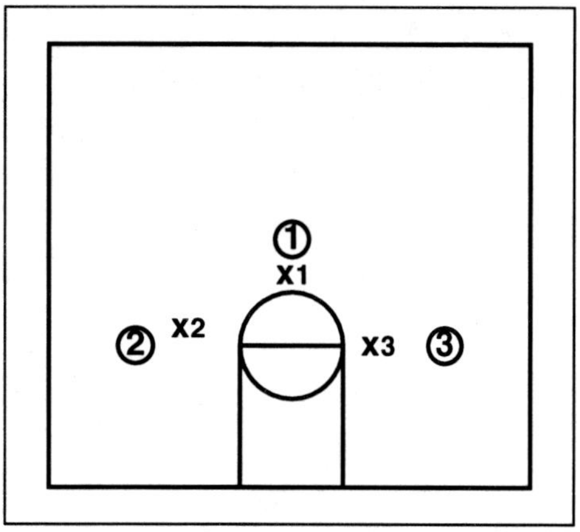

Diagram 11-8

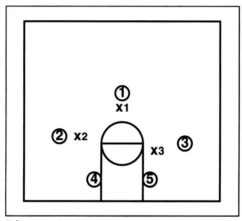

Diagram 11-9

Positions: 1, 2, 3
Number of Players: 8
Time: 9 minutes

Description:
- Three phases are used to teach your half-court perimeter players to play your offense. Motion options will be used to demonstrate the three phases.
- The first phase utilizes three perimeter attackers versus no defenders. For three minutes, the perimeter players run their options without taking a shot. You can require them to talk if you wish. Each perimeter player has four options in the motion offense:

✓ Screen away.

✓ V-cut to replace himself.

✓ Dribble toward a player, compelling that player to fade cut.

✓ Cut to the basket and go to either corner before reentering the offense.

- The second phase puts three defenders on the three perimeter attackers (Diagram 11-8). For three minutes, this phase is executed under live game conditions. You may rotate offense to defense to offense as many times as you wish. Or you may use the strategies of Drill #143.

- In the third phase, post players (4 and 5 in Diagram 11-9) are added. The two post players execute their movement without defenders. The two post players cannot shoot or try to score. They serve as outlet receivers should the three perimeter attackers be unable to free themselves for scores. This phase should be run for three minutes.

- You can add the post players with no defenders to the first phase where the perimeter players have no defenders.

Variations:

- Designate a certain player to score. Doing so compels the other players to set more screens, and so forth, to get that player open. Do not let the defense know who that scorer will be.

- Designate that scoring can only occur off certain types of partial play(s) (for example, only off backdoor cuts). Do not let the defense know which option(s) will be used.

Rotations: Make sure all players who will play the perimeter get to play those positions during this drill.

Drill #142: Half-Court Post Offense

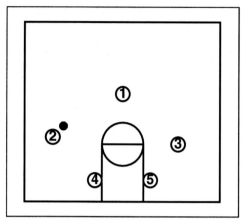

Diagram 11-10

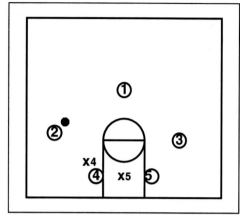

Diagram 11-11

Positions: 4, 5
Number of Players: 7
Time: 8 minutes

Description:

- Two phases are used to teach your half-court post players to play your offense. Motion options will be used to demonstrate the two phases.
- The first phase uses two post attackers versus no defenders. For four minutes, the post players run their options without taking a shot. You can begin the drill by having the perimeter players stand still while the post players work on their options. Then you can have the perimeter players run their options while the post players work on theirs. You can require them to talk if you wish. Each post player has seven options in the motion offense:
  - ✓ Screen away for other post player.
  - ✓ Work hard for post positioning on his defender.
  - ✓ Screen for a perimeter player.
  - ✓ Flash-pivot cut to high post.
  - ✓ Move to short corner, especially against zone defenses.
  - ✓ Run a curl move from short corner.
  - ✓ Work high-low post options with other post player.
- The second phase puts two defenders on the two post attackers (Diagram 11-11). For four minutes, this phase is executed under live game conditions. You may rotate offense to defense to offense as many times as you wish, or you may use the strategies outlined in Drill #143.

Variations:

- Designate a certain player to score. Doing so compels the other players to set more screens, and so forth, to get that player open. Do not let the defense know who that scorer will be.
- Designate scoring can only occur off certain types of partial play(s) (for example, scoring only by a post player who first must seal his defender). Do not let the defense know which option(s) will be used.

Rotations: Make sure all players who will play the post get to play those positions during this drill.

Drill #143: Five-on-Five Control Scrimmages

Positions: 1, 2, 3, 4, 5
Number of Players: 10
Time: 10 minutes or more

Procedure:

- Scrimmage can be approached in many ways under control situations (offensive rebounding is allowed under all of these options):
  - ✓ To stay on offense, a team must score a number of consecutive baskets before they are allowed not to score (start season with two consecutive and work up to four).
  - ✓ To stay on offense, the team must score in the last second of the drill (simulating winning the game on last possession). You may run this strategy while running any of the other strategies.
  - ✓ Have a set number of scores: two out of three and you get to stay on offense (or three out of five; etc.).
  - ✓ Give one team the ball 10 times. Give the other team the ball 10 times. See which team scores the greatest percentage.
  - ✓ Divide the 10 minutes into two phases of five minutes each. Give each squad the ball for five minutes. Keep the score on the clock and see who wins.
  - ✓ This strategy can be used with all the previously mentioned tactics. Fast break on all defensive rebounds, or break the press on all made shots. Then reset on the other end of the court, and begin the drill again.
  - ✓ Designate a certain player to score (or two players—a perimeter player and a post player makes for a great tactic). All the other teammates will have to work hard to get those players open, especially when the team must score two out of three times to keep the ball. Do not tell the defense who those designees are. From time to time, you can tell the defense, which really compels the offense and the defense to work exceptionally hard. When you do tell the defense, allow any offensive player to score when he gets a wide open lay-up.
  - ✓ Designate that a score must occur off of a certain type of offensive option, like off of a screen. You can even make the designation two options if you wish. The offense may score off either option. Again, do not tell the defense.
  - ✓ Have one team working on the half-court offense while the other team works on fast breaking or breaking the press (if the basket is scored).

About the Author

Burrall Paye is a retired coach with 37 years of experience. He began his coaching career at Whittle Springs Junior High School in Knoxville, Tennessee, where he coached boys' basketball and baseball. Both of Paye's teams (basketball and baseball) won the district and regional championships his first year. Prior to Paye's tenure, Whittle Springs had never had a winning record in any sport.

After nine years, Burrall moved to Powell Valley High School in Big Stone Gap, Virginia, where he coached both boys' and girls' basketball. His first team at Powell Valley not only won the district championship, but it advanced to the quarterfinals of the state tournament. During his eight years at Powell Valley, Paye's teams won 24 different championships, including an undefeated state championship in boys' basketball and an undefeated regional championship in girls' basketball (girls did not play beyond the regional level at that time). Before Paye's arrival, Powell Valley had never won a district championship in any sport in the entire history of the school. Since Paye departed, Powell Valley's girls' and boys' basketball teams have returned to the state tournament only once in 31 years.

In 1977, Paye moved to William Fleming High School in Roanoke, Virginia. William Fleming had been to the regionals only twice in the preceding 25 years. During the next 18 years, William Fleming would advance to the regional semifinals or beyond 17 consecutive times, winning 25 different championships, including five regional championships and seven trips to the state final four. Paye's Fleming teams played against and defeated some of the great high school programs in the United States, including Oak Hill Academy, voted by USA Today as the number one program in the USA in the last 25 years.

During Paye's career, his teams won 764 games, losing only 196. His teams won 64 different championships, earning the coach 42 different coach of the year awards, including state coach of the year (twice) and the National Federation Interscholastic Association Outstanding Coach of the Year award. He has coached in the annual allstar game in Virginia nine times.

Since his retirement in 1996, Paye has continued to teach basketball through his writings and his clinics. He has spoken at most of the major basketball clinics in the

United States, Canada, Europe, and Latin America. He was the featured speaker at the National High School Association annual convention in New Orleans, Louisiana, in 1987. He has written 10 full-length basketball books and hundreds of articles for national basketball magazines.

Paye graduated from Lincoln Memorial University in Harrogate, Tennessee, in 1958 and received his masters degree from the University of Tennessee in 1965. He is married to Nancy Sturgill and lives in Roanoke, Virginia. He has one son, Patrick, who is a highly successful high school basketball coach in North Carolina.

Patrick Paye, Burrall's son, is currently the head boy's basketball coach at Northeastern High School in Elizabeth City, North Carolina. Patrick has never been part of a losing season as a player (in his collegiate playing career) or a coach (17 years of coaching at the college and high school levels). He has rebuilt two traditionally losing programs into playoff teams during his career as a high school coach. Northeastern has won the sectional championship in three of the last four years, advancing to the Elite Eight of the state of North Carolina, and has made the state playoffs eight consecutive years. Patrick and his son, Rylan, reside in Grandy, North Carolina.